MINNESOTA
IN THE
CIVIL WAR

MINNESOTA IN THE CIVIL WAR

By KENNETH CARLEY

Ross & Haines, Inc.

Minneapolis - 1961 - Minnesota

To Lucile

CONTENTS

ACKNOWLEDGEMENTS . . .

We wish to express our thanks for the co-operation of the Minneapolis Star and Tribune Company, who have kindly granted permission for the use of Mr. Carley's material in book form. Many of these chapters first appeared in Picture Magazine which is issued as part of the Minneapolis Sunday Tribune.

We also wish to extend our thanks to the Minnesota Civil War and Sioux Uprising Commission for allowing the use of the CHRONOLOGY which Mr. Carley originally prepared for their use.

THE PUBLISHERS

June, 1961

INTRODUCTION

Among paintings in the governor's reception room
and its anteroom in the Minnesota state capitol
in St. Paul are six large canvases depicting Minnesota regiments during memorable moments in
the Civil war.

The building was brand new in the spring of
1905 when the state board of capitol commis-
sioners, apparently yielding to the wishes of the
Grand Army of the Republic and other patriotic
groups, decided that capitol decorations should
include four Civil war pictures. The board arranged for noted artists of the time to do the First
Minnesota at Gettysburg, the Second Minnesota
at Missionary ridge, the Fourth Minnesota at
Vicksburg and Minnesota troops at Nashville.

The first Civil war picture to be hung (in the
fall of 1906) was "The Battle of Nashville,"
by famed illustrator Howard Pyle. It has been
widely acclaimed an outstanding war painting.
Douglas Volk's Missionary ridge painting was
hung soon after and was followed in due time
by Rufus H. Zogbaum's "The Battle of Gettysburg" and Francis D. Millet's "The Fourth Minnesota Regiment Entering Vicksburg."

It was not until 1911 and 1912 that Stanley M.

Arthurs' "The Third Minnesota Regiment Entering Little Rock" and Edwin H. Blashfield's "The Fifth Minnesota Regiment at Corinth" were added to the original four.

All six paintings are reproduced in color in the following pages along with fairly extensive articles that background actions pictured. Although one might wish for a painting of the Second Minnesota regiment at Chickamauga, or of the First Minnesota battery at Shiloh, or of the Eighth Minnesota regiment at Murfreesboro, it is indeed fortunate that so much of Minnesota's Civil war history has been done in picture form. The paintings and the accompanying text leave some gaps, but together they present most of the important phases of the state's Civil war story.

Minnesota became a state in 1858 and thus was only a "youngster" when war broke out. Nevertheless, from 22,000 to 25,000 of Minnesota's men answered the call to arms during the war. Grouped into eleven infantry regiments, some light artillery batteries and a few other units, they fought Confederates and disease in the south and east and Sioux Indians at home. At least 2,500 Minnesotans died in the war. More populous states furnished many more soldiers than Minnesota did, of course, but Minnesotans, it seems, had a flair for being in the right place at the right time. They appear to have had a hand in crucial fighting more often than their limited numbers would warrant.

The following accounts purposely focus on Minnesotans, but in most instances readers should keep in mind that Minnesota troops shared their moments of glory with men of other states who were just as deserving of praise or mention.

The text backgrounding the paintings in this book is an amplified version of a series of articles that first appeared in the Minneapolis Sunday Tribune's Picture magazine as a Civil War Centennial feature.

More people than can be mentioned here have helped me. However, I want especially to acknowledge the assistance of the following on the Minnesota Historical society staff: Lois Fawcett, chief reference librarian, who came up with answers to what must have seemed endless questions; Eugene D. Becker, picture curator; Helene M. Thomson, assistant picture curator; Lucile Kane, manuscripts curator, and her staff; Thomas Deahl, newspaper curator; Russell W. Fridley, director, and Robert C. Wheeler, assistant director.

Helpful, too, were: Edwin C. Bearss, research historian at Vicksburg national military park; Rock L. Comstock Jr., historian at Chickamauga and Chattanooga national military park, and Frederick E. Tilberg, historian at Gettysburg national military park. A prime source for the chapter on Nashville was Stanley F. Horn's authoritative book, "The Decisive Battle of Nashville." Hugh Walker, feature editor of The Nashville Tennessean, kindly lent some Nashville material.

G. S. Petterson, curator of Blue Earth County Historical society, Mankato, furnished quotes from the letters of Billings J. Sibley of the Second Minnesota. Among descendants of Minnesota soldiers who furnished—or offered—material was

B. M. Ahsenmacher of Minneapolis, who provided a copy of the diary of his grandfather, Sgt. Henry Ahsenmacher of the 10th Minnesota.

I am grateful to all these people, as well as to Charles McFadden, editor of Picture magazine, who freed me for Civil war "service." Thanks also go to my "widowed" wife and our three daughters for their patience and assistance and to fellow members of the Twin Cities Civil War Round Table for suggestions, criticism and encouragement.

Minneapolis
June, 1961

KENNETH CARLEY

"Do you see those colors? Then take them!" ordered Gen. Winfield S. Hancock (sword extended) at a critical moment late in the afternoon of July 2, 1863, at Gettysburg, Pa. Receiving the order is Col. William Colvill of the First Minnesota. A few moments later Colvill was wounded leading his men in the famous sacrificial charge that saved the Union center but cost the regiment 82 per cent of its men. Minnesota Historical Society

GALLANTRY AT GETTYSBURG

CIVIL WAR BROKE OUT in the east in the spring of 1861 and quickly touched distant Minnesota. Alexander Ramsey, the young state's enterprising governor, was in Washington April 13 when ominous news raced through the capital. Fort Sumter, federal bastion off Charleston, S. C., had surrendered!

The next morning Ramsey hurried to the office of Secretary of War Simon Cameron, an old

MINNESOTA IN THE CIVIL WAR

Pennsylvania colleague of his, and offered 1,000 soldiers for national defense. Cameron was about to leave for a conference with President Lincoln and said he would present the offer if Ramsey would write it out. Ramsey did so and Lincoln accepted the tender, the first received by the government. By telegraph, Ramsey put in motion a chain of events at home that soon had 10 companies of the First Regiment of Minnesota Volunteers training at Fort Snelling.

The regiment originally was organized on a 90-day basis in keeping with President Abraham Lincoln's April 15 call for 75,000 volunteers to serve for three months. But on May 3 Lincoln appealed for 42,000 volunteers for three years or longer, so the First Minnesota was organized as the senior three-year regiment of the war.

When the call went out for troops, Minnesota had been a state only three years. What it lacked in numbers (its 1860 population was but 172,-023), it made up in an initial burst of patriotism. Public meetings in various towns stirred up lots of enthusiasm and helped produce more than enough recruits.

Farm boys, shopkeepers, lumberjacks, professional men and many others signed up "to defend the flag and suppress the rebellion." The names of the various volunteer companies, which also were given the usual letter designations A through K (except for J), indicate some of the areas the men came from:

Minnesota Pioneer Guards (St. Paul), St. Paul Volunteers, Stillwater G u a r d s, St. Anthony

Zouaves, Lincoln Guards, Goodhue Volunteers, Faribault Volunteers, Dakota Volunteers, Wabasha Volunteers, Winona Volunteers.

Who were some of these early volunteers? One was Josias R. King, St. Paul surveyor. He was the first to sign an agreement to enlist when the Pioneer Guards met the evening of April 15 and thus always claimed (in spite of opposition) that he was the first Union volunteer in the war.

Then there was a young farm boy named Newton Brown who afterward recalled that he walked 65 miles barefooted to St. Paul from Waterville, Minn., to enlist. Another young farmer, John O. Milne, came from Lebanon in Dakota county to enlist in company I. He would have a harrowing experience at Bull Run.

A Winona leather store clerk, Matthew Marvin, enlisted in company K and kept a diary that is a good source of information about such actions as the Minnesota charge at Gettysburg, where Marvin was wounded.

Patrick Henry Taylor, a schoolteacher at Little Falls and other Morrison county settlements, enlisted in company E. His brother Isaac came up from Illinois to take Henry's place as a teacher but before long also enlisted and caught up with the regiment in the east. Isaac kept an important diary that details what the First Minnesota did from January 1862 until the Gettysburg charge, in which Isaac was killed.

Then there was Alfred Carpenter, a Winona county farm hand who enlisted at St. Charles, Minn., and would write a dramatic letter about

17

Leader of the Minnesotans' charge, William Colvill of Red Wing, was the regiment's fifth colonel. Willis A. Gorman, Napoleon J. T. Dana, Alfred Sully and George N. Morgan preceded him as head of the regiment. Colvill is honored by statues in the rotunda of the state capitol and at his grave in Cannon Falls, Minn.   Minnesota Historical Society

Gettysburg after the battle. We will meet these various recruits, briefly, later.

Named colonel of the First Minnesota was a former governor of Minnesota territory, Willis A. Gorman. Among other officers was William Colvill, Jr., of Red Wing, who would work his way up to colonel of the regiment during its most shining hours at Gettysburg.

Many of the men had had militia training, so it wasn't too hard to forge them into a crack regiment that could march and drill with precision. Their uniforms must have been something to behold. The citizens of Winona furnished company K some neat gray outfits but the rest wore

18

a state-furnished array of red flannel shirts, black trousers, black felt hats and socks. The men didn't get regular army uniforms till August.

Early weeks in the army were like one long holiday for the men of the First Minnesota. Few people expected the war to last long. On May 21 the regiment marched to a grove on Nicollet island in the Mississippi to be banqueted by the ladies of St. Anthony and Minneapolis. Five days later, in a ceremony at the state capitol, the women of St. Paul presented the regiment a flag it carried through its term of service.

Although allowed these and other outings, the men of the First Minnesota learned that Col. Gorman, a veteran of the Mexican war, was an efficient officer who enforced discipline. For this he earned their cordial hatred at first but later on when they got into the war they could see that Gorman had done them a favor.

Orders arrived June 14 for the regiment to go to Washington. Early on June 22 the Rev. Edward D. Neill, chaplain, conducted religious services at Fort Snelling, a f t e r which the men marched through St. Paul streets "thronged by a sympathetic and enthusiastic multitude." Then the regiment embarked on steamers for the trip to La Crosse and Prairie du Chien, Wis., where the men boarded railroad cars for Chicago. There, a large crowd and Mayor John Wentworth greeted the regiment as it mached from one railroad station to another.

The next day the Chicago Tribune rhapsodized: "There are few regiments we have ever seen that can compare in brawn and muscle with these Minnesotans, used to the axe, the rifle, the oar and the setting pole. They are un-questionably the finest body of troops that has yet appeared in our streets."

The same pattern of cheering crowds con-tinued all the way to Washington, except for a tense moment or two in hostile Baltimore, Md. After "touring" the nation's capital, the regiment settled down July 3 to drilling and picket duty in a camp near Alexandria, Va. There it became part of Col. W. B. Franklin's brigade of Col. S. P. Heintzelman's division.

Then, suddenly, the war ceased being a "lark" and became nasty business. On July 21, 1861, a month lacking a day after it left Fort Snelling, the First Minnesota regiment got its baptism of fire in the battle of First Bull Run (Manassas), Va., a Union disaster. The Minnesotans, who boasted they were among the few northerners to retire from the field in good order, lost 42 men killed, 108 wounded and 30 missing—about 20 per cent of the men engaged.

One of the wounded was the "barefoot re-cruit," Newton Brown. Another was J. O. Milne, who was left for dead after the battle and lay "dimly conscious from loss of blood" for 48 hours before a Confederate burial party picked him up. He was "jarred" in great pain to Richmond, Va., in a train of cattle cars. In the Confederate capital Milne had the good fortune to meet another prisoner, Dr. J. H. Stewart of St. Paul, the regi-mental surgeon. Stewart dressed Milne's wounds and helped him recover sufficiently to be exchanged. Later, Milne served two terms in the Minnesota state senate and became a leading citizen of Duluth.

For the First Minnesota the two years that followed Bull Run moved toward a climax at Gettysburg with the inevitability of a Greek tragedy. Several rigorous campaigns helped shape the regiment into one of the best of the entire Army of the Potomac. It became, in fact, just the kind of outfit that could be counted on to meet almost any test in an emergency.

Hard service with the army's proud second corps (of which the regiment was part of the first brigade, second division) also greatly reduced the First Minnesota's numbers. In one of the Seven Days' battles at Savage's Station, Va., June 29, 1862, for instance, the regiment lost 48 killed and wounded during important rear-guard action while the Army of the Potomac retreated towards the James river during the Peninsular campaign.

The bloodiest single day of the war near Antietam creek in Maryland Sept. 17, 1862, saw the First Minnesota lose 147 more killed and wounded. The regiment took part in one of the piecemeal attacks that marked the north's frustrating offensive that day. Other actions cost the First Minnesota more men.

Thus it was that the regiment was much under its original strength of nearly 1,000 men when it accompanied the rest of the Army of the Potomac northward through Virginia and Maryland in June 1863. Gen. Robert E. Lee was leading his Army of Northern Virginia on a second invasion of the north, and the Army of the Potomac made a parallel move, keeping between Lee and Washington.

A long, exhausting march in intense heat brought the regiment near Frederick, Md., June 28. The next day the regiment suffered the indignity of having its colonel, William Colvill, arrested. He had been "insubordinate" for letting some of his men scurry dry-shod across timbers over a creek when they were supposed to keep in the ranks and wade right through the water. One regimental historian commented: "This act produced a strong feeling of resentment in the men, who felt that their colonel was most unjustly dealt with."

Some also were unhappy to learn that, with a major battle obviously shaping up, the army's top command had been shifted. Dour Gen. George G. Meade replaced Gen. Joseph Hooker, who had headed the Army of the Potomac since January. Diarist Isaac Taylor said the news of the change "falls on us 'like a wet blanket.' "

The men, however, took comfort from the fact that on July 1 Meade sent their popular corps commander—handsome, soldierly Gen. Winfield S. Hancock—ahead to Gettysburg, Pa., to take temporary command and decide whether Union forces should attempt a stand there. The men could hear the distant artillery of the first day's battle at Gettysburg July 1 as they moved up. That night the First Minnesota encamped four miles south of town while Hancock organized the fishhook-shaped Union defense line along Culp's hill, Cemetery hill and Cemetery ridge just south of Gettysburg.

Aroused at daybreak July 2, the First Minnesota arrived on the field about 5:45 a.m. and soon welcomed Col. Colvill, who had been released from arrest. Most of the second corps took position as the Union center on Cemetery ridge. To the left was the third corps, commanded by a New York politican, Gen. Daniel E. Sickles. For some reason the First Minnesota was detached and held in reserve a short distance to the rear.

The Union line on the left, as well as part of the center, was badly disorganized in the afternoon when Sickles suddenly advanced his third corps half a mile or more to high ground at the Peach Orchard near the Emmitsburg road. Meanwhile, Confederate Gen. James Longstreet, on the right of the Rebel line on Seminary ridge to the west, finally hit the Union left in attacks Lee had hoped would take place earlier. Hours of confused, touch-and-go fighting produced staggering losses and several crises on the Union left in places that now rate capital letters—Little Round Top, the Wheat Field, Devil's Den, among others. Sickles' salient, particularly, was in a bad way from Rebel attacks but Hancock was able to come to the rescue by dispersing units in his corps.

The First Minnesota was sent to the center of the field on Cemetery ridge to support a battery. Minus three companies on skirmish duty, the Minnesotans numbered but 262 officers and men. About an hour before sunset the First Minnesota from its vantage point could see perhaps the worst crisis of the afternoon developing out in front of it near the Emmitsburg road. Gen. A. A. Humphreys' division of Sickles' corps broke under Confederate assaults and raced in disorder back to the main Union lines, passing the position of the First Minnesota.

Into the gap poured two Confederate brigades of Gen. A. P. Hill's corps—Alabamians commanded by Gen. Cadmus Wilcox and Florida troops led by Col. David Lang. They would crack the Union center if they weren't soon stopped.

Desperate for a little time to patch up the ranks with reserves he had ordered up, Hancock spied the First Minnesota. He galloped over to Colvill and shouted, "What regiment is this?"

"First Minnesota," Colvill answered.

"Colonel, do you see those colors?" asked Hancock, pointing to the Confederate attackers. Colvill said he did. "Then take them!" ordered Hancock. (Another version has Hancock ordering, "Charge those lines!")

The men plunged ahead without flinching, although they knew they were being sacrificed to buy maybe five minutes' time. The Minnesotans rushed down the slope through the din, the smoke, the deepening shadows. There was no stopping to fire, but men soon started falling.

"Bullets whistled past us; shells screeched over us; canister and grape fell about us; comrade after comrade dropped from the ranks; but on the line went"—so wrote one of the wounded attackers, Alfred Carpenter, in an eloquent letter

24

three weeks later.

"Charge!" shouted Colvill as the men neared the first Confederate line in a ravine. Bayonets lowered, the regiment struck at a fortunate moment when the Confederates were slightly disordered while crossing a dry brook at the foot of the slope. The force of the charge drove the first Confederate line back on the second line. Using the low banks of the dry brook for shelter, the Minnesotans then poured a volley into the Confederates, arresting the whole attack long enough to give Hancock the time he had to have to bring

This is an artist's drawing of the charging First Minnesota regiment rushing down a field toward the ravine where it met oncoming Confederates at Gettysburg. What the men lacked in numbers they made up in determination. At fearful cost, they stemmed the southerners' attack.

Minnesota Historical Society

up reserves. The Union center was saved.

Wrote Bruce Catton in "Glory Road": "The whole war had suddenly come to a focus in this smoky hollow, with a few score westerners trading their lives for the time the army needed . . . They had not captured the flag that Hancock had asked them to capture, but they still had their own flag and a great name . . ."

One small regiment, however brave, couldn't hope to hold out very long against two brigades. Confederate fire from three sides soon took a dreadful toll. Within 15 minutes, 215 of the 262 men who made the charge lay dead or wounded. Colvill and all his field officers were struck down. Only 47 attackers returned unscathed. The rate of loss in the charge—82 per cent—usually is cited as the largest suffered in any regiment in the entire war. Said Lt. Col. Joseph B. Mitchell in his "Decisive Battles of the Civil War": "There is no other unit in the history of warfare that ever made such a charge and then stood its ground sustaining such losses."

After the Confederates retreated and the fighting died down, surviving Minnesotans gathered their wounded comrades in the darkness. Matthew Marvin was shot in the heel and wrote in his diary afterward that he fainted twice from pain and loss of blood. He managed to crawl back on his hands and knees until a colleague assisted him.

Schoolteacher Henry Taylor supervised removal of wounded Col. Colvill and others from the field. Then Henry looked in vain for his brother Isaac. Not until the next morning did he find Isaac—dead. He buried him. No longer would Isaac's diary detail the record of the First Minnesota.

But there was still more fighting for the regiment. The next day (July 3) the First Minnesota's remnant, augmented by the companies that had been detached as skirmishers, lost another 17 killed or wounded while helping beat back the attack known as "Pickett's charge" against the Union center. The three-day battle ended with this climactic action.

The following Oct. 14 the regiment suffered another 17 casualties in action at Bristoe Station,

This photograph by Alexander Gardner shows some of the dead of the First Minnesota at Gettysburg. The regiment suffered 215 killed and wounded out of the 262 who made the charge. Late in the evening of July 2, the 47 survivors had the grim job of rescuing wounded and locating dead in the dark. The next day the regiment lost another 17 killed and wounded during the repulse of Pickett's charge.
Library of Congress

Va., on the Orange & Alexandria railroad. The Minnesotans captured 322 Confederates here— more than their own number. The story goes that some of the captives had been up against the second division of the second corps (to which the First Minnesota belonged) at Gettysburg. When they saw the division's white trefoil badge on the Minnesotans, the captured Confederates are said to have exclaimed: "Here's those damned white clubs again!"

In February 1864 the First Minnesota headed for home after being honored in Washington at a banquet at which the regiment's tattered battle flags served as table decorations. Most of the men were mustered out at Fort Snelling April 29, although some re-enlisted. In percentage of total enrollment killed during the war, the First Minnesota ranked 23rd out of 2,047 Federal regiments.

Many tributes came the First Minnesota's way but none more heartfelt than Gen. Winfield S. Hancock's. In a conversation with Minnesota's Sen. Morton S. Wilkinson, he said of the Gettysburg charge: "I had no alternative but to order the regiment in. We had no force on hand to meet the sudden emergency. Troops had been ordered up and were coming on the run, but I saw that in some way five minutes must be gained or we were lost. It was fortunate that I found there so grand a body of men as the First Minnesota. I knew they must lose heavily and it caused me pain to give the order for them to advance, but I would have done it if I had known every man would be killed. It was a sacrifice that must be made. The superb gallantry of those men saved our line from being broken. No soldiers, on any field, in this or any other country, ever displayed grander heroism."

This is the way a member of the regiment, Josias R. King of St. Paul, pictured the dramatic scene when the First Minnesota got the order to charge onrushing Confederates about 7 p.m., July 2, 1863. Gen. Winfield S. Hancock (on horse, pointing) is shown commanding Col. William Colvill (on foot in this version) to make the attack. King, a surveyor, was a member of the St. Paul Pioneer Guards and claimed to be the first Union volunteer.

Courtesy William G. Kreger, Jackson, Minnesota

This monument on Cemetery ridge commemorates the celebrated charge of the First Minnesota regiment at Gettysburg. Unveiled in 1897 on the 34th anniversary of the regiment's attack, the monument stands near the Pennsylvania memorial, largest on the field. The 10-foot-high bronze statue that surmounts the monument's granite base was done by sculptor Jacob H. G. Fjelde, who is better known for his Ole Bull statue in Minneapolis.

Artist's version of the Second Minnesota's division (Baird's) capturing Confederate guns on the left atop Missionary ridge.

STORMING MISSIONARY RIDGE

AROUND THE MOUNTAIN fastness of Chattanooga, Tenn., in the late summer and fall of 1863 were fought some of the Civil war's most dramatic battles. Playing a commendable role in them was the Second Minnesota regiment, a seasoned outfit with two years of hard service already behind it.

The Second Minnesota, then led by Col. Horatio P. Van Cleve, was one of four regiments that bore the brunt of fighting at Mill Springs, Ky., Jan. 19, 1862. The first battle for the Second Minnesota, it was a Union victory. During remaining months of 1862 the regiment did con-

"The Battle of Gettysburg," by Rufus H. Zogbaum, depicts famous charge of the First Minnesota.

"The Second Minnesota Regiment at Missionary Ridge," by Douglas Volk, shows Lt. Col. Judson W. Bishop (hat in hand) urging men on.

Stanley M. Arthurs

"The Third Minnesota Regiment Entering Little Rock," by Stanley M. Arthurs.

"The Fourth Minnesota Regiment Entering Vicksburg," by Francis D. Millet.

"The Fifth Minnesota Regiment at Corinth," by Edwin H. Blashfield.

"The Battle of Nashville," by Howard Pyle, pictures Minnesotans' crucial attack on Shy's hill.

siderable marching in Kentucky, Tennessee and Mississippi while taking part in the Corinth and Perryville campaigns.

Both north and south realized the importance of Chattanooga as the gateway to the heart of the Confederacy or, conversely, to eastern Tennessee and Kentucky. A web of railroads and roads made Chattanooga a vital communications hub. So did the navigable Tennessee river which wound past the city's "doorstep" while looping through a gap in the Cumberland mountains.

The previous July the divided nation's attention had been on both Gettysburg, Pa., and Vicksburg, Miss.

Then, in September, the main spotlight of war switched to the Chattanooga area. The first "round" of the struggle for Chattanooga went to the Confederates Sept. 19-20 along Chickamauga creek, about 10 miles south of the city. There, in some of the fiercest fighting of the war, 66,000 Confederates under irritable, unpopular Gen. Braxton Bragg defeated the Union Army of the Cumberland, which numbered about 58,000 and was led by Gen. William S. (Old Rosy) Rosecrans. The Confederate force was primarily the Army of Tennessee, but it was reinforced by the late arrival of most of Gen. James Longstreet's corps from Virginia.

The first day's fighting at Chickamauga was bloody but inconclusive. On the 20th, however, Longstreet had the good luck to attack at the exact spot where a mix-up had created a gap in the Federal lines. The Confederates drove the

Union right flank back and sent Rosecrans and much of his army packing for Chattanooga.

Rosecrans and several of his generals thought the entire Army of the Cumberland had been destroyed, but fortunately for the north one of the army's corps commanders saved the day at Chickamauga. He was Gen. George H. Thomas, a stolid Virginian who headed the Union 14th corps, to which the Second Minnesota belonged.

Thomas rallied the Minnesotans and several other regiments on Snodgrass hill and made a heroic stand there against repeated Confederate attacks. Not until 7:30 p.m. did the Minnesotans' brigade (Col. Ferdinand Van Derveer's) leave the ridge and head for Chattanooga. Thomas ever after was known as "the Rock of Chickamauga."

At Chickamauga the Confederates lost 18,000 killed, wounded or missing and the Union army had 16,000 casualties. The Second Minnesota, which fought in at least three places during the two days' battle, had 45 killed, 103 wounded and 14 captured—162 out of 384 engaged.

Although Chickamauga was a southern victory, Bragg failed to follow up effectively and thereby lost much of his advantage. Many of Bragg's subordinates thought he should be replaced, but President Jefferson Davis kept him in command.

But Bragg did bottle up Rosecrans' Army of the Cumberland in Chattanooga. The Confederates besieged the city, hoping to starve the northerners into surrender. The southerners occupied Lookout mountain, a 1,500-foot-high escarpment overlooking a huge U-shaped bend of the river southwest of the city. They also fortified Missionary ridge—a long range rising 200 to 500 feet above the plain east and southeast of the city—and took over the valley between the mountain fortresses. Few battles have had as spectacular a setting as those that soon took place around Chattanooga.

Confederate possession of high ground cut off practically all the Union supply lines. Only a trickle of food and other necessities got through. Before long the northern army was reduced to half rations. Thousands of mules and other animals died of starvation and the human sick list got long. The Second Minnesota, of course, suffered along with the rest of the men during the two-month siege.

Then matters slowly improved. Gen. Ulysses S. Grant was promoted to command of the armies of the west and on Oct. 23 arrived at Chattanooga to take personal charge of the situation there. Thomas replaced Rosecrans as commander of the Army of the Cumberland; Gen. William T. Sherman took Grant's place as head of the Army of the Tennessee and set out for Chattanooga with part of that army. Gen. Joseph Hooker also was dispatched to Chattanooga with a detachment from the celebrated Army of the Potomac, pride of the east.

Reorganization of the Army of the Cumberland now put the Second Minnesota and the rest of Van Derveer's brigade in Gen. Absalom Baird's division (the third) of the 14th corps.

In the last week of October a water-land supply

line again was opened to the west, thanks in part to the efforts of a prominent Minnesotan in the quartermaster c o r p s—William G. LeDuc of Hastings. Now the gaunt Union troops at Chattanooga began to enjoy full rations once more. November was well along, though, before all the northern forces arrived and Grant could set in motion his plan for breaking out of the Chattanooga impasse.

When that plan unfolded, the men of the Army of the Cumberland did a burn. Still smarting under the loss of prestige at Chickamauga, the Cumberlanders could see that in the coming battle Grant would have them playing second fiddle to Hooker's easterners and Sherman's westerners.

On Nov. 24, Hooker's army dislodged the Confederate left on Lookout mountain, defeating the small southern force there in a lofty engagement romanticized as "the battle above the clouds." These Confederates retreated eastward and joined the main force under Bragg on Missionary ridge.

Grant called for Sherman to make the principal attack on the Confederate right and on the 24th he crossed the Tennessee river and assaulted what he thought was the north end of Missionary ridge. Actually, Sherman's men captured a separate hill and still faced the prospect of attacking Missionary ridge from the north. This they did Nov. 25 but they made little progress against the stubborn Confederates. Hooker was supposed to make a diversionary attack on the other end of the ridge but was delayed.

Meanwhile, Thomas' Army of the Cumberland

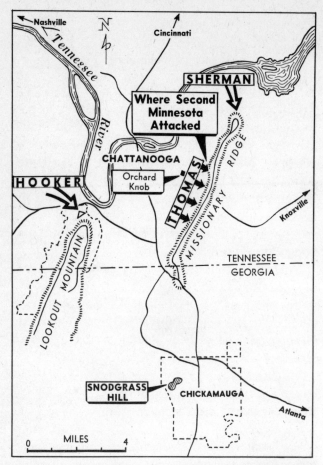

Map by Warner Nelson

(including the Second Minnesota) was arranged in double lines on the plain about a mile in front of the fortified center of the enemy on Missionary ridge. The Confederate position ahead was formidable. The ridge was steep, craggy, wooded and cut by Confederate entrenchments at the foot and halfway up. The crest bristled with Confederate guns. Normally, no troops could be expected to carry such a stronghold by frontal attack.

Grant, headquartered on a nearby height called Orchard Knob, could see that Sherman was mak-

ing little or no progress with the main attack on
the north end of the ridge. As the afternoon wore
on, he ordered Thomas to ease the pressure on
Sherman by having the Army of the Cumberland
make a limited attack on the Confederate center.
The Cumberlanders, at a six-gun signal, were to
take only the first line of Confederate rifle pits at
the base of the ridge. Then they were to stop and
await orders. Still chafing at what they considered
an attempt to teach them an "object lesson,"
Thomas' men swept towards the ridge. They com-
prised four divisions plus artillery—some 20,000
men in 60 regiments, including the Second Minnesota. (Pickett had only 15,000 men in the more
famous Confederate charge at Gettysburg.)

The Minnesotans' colonel, James George of
Rochester, had left for home a few days earlier
because of chronic ill health, so the regiment was
led by Lt. Col. Judson W. Bishop, 32, former
railroad man who was editor of the Chatfield
Democrat when war broke out. Bishop headed
the regiment during the rest of its war service
and became its historian.

As the men approached the ridge, the Second
Minnesota's division (Baird's) was on the left.
The regiment's brigade (Van Derveer's) was in
the center of the division and was formed for
battle in two lines of three regiments each. The
Second Minnesota was in advance, covering the
whole brigade front, with two companies deployed
as skirmishers. At about 4 p.m., Bishop was ordered to lead the Minnesotans in a desperate
charge against Confederates posted in rifle pits

49

on a secondary ridge that lay a short distance in front of the main ridge. The Second Minnesota drove the southerners back and held the position under artillery fire for 20 minutes until the rest of the brigade came up.

Then followed one of the war's most amazing episodes—one made to order for a present day Hollywood scenario writer. As they were supposed to, Thomas' divisions successfully stormed the first Confederate line at the bottom. A mass inspiration then seemed to hit all 20,000 attackers

This monument on Missionary ridge commemorates the Second Minnesota's capture of rifle pits at the foot and its part in the main assault.

Chattanooga-Chickamauga National Military Park

at once. Without orders, and in spite of some officers' efforts to stop them, the men continued right up the steep side of Missionary ridge. Rising irresistibly like floodwaters, the Federals clambered after the Confederates. There were shouts of "Chickamauga!" Southern guns took their toll— especially of regimental color bearers—but the surge upward continued. The men sought cover where they could, and regiments got mixed up, but nothing stopped the impetus of the drive.

Back on Orchard Knob, Grant was astounded at what he saw. He is said to have turned to his generals and demanded: "Who ordered those men up the hill?" No one seemed to know. Grant is reported to have said: "Someone will suffer for it if it turns out badly."

But he needn't have worried. The unordered "soldier's battle" had become a great "soldier's victory." The Federals roared over the top, many of the regiments planting their colors on the crest at about the same time. They captured guns and some enemy soldiers and sent most of Bragg's army in pell-mell retreat in the direction of Dalton, Ga., to the south.

The triumph was complete and glorious, but an "assist" should be credited to the ineptness of Bragg. Earlier, Bragg had weakened his lines on Missionary ridge by sending Longstreet to attack Federals at Knoxville, Tenn. The remaining Confederate troops were faultily disposed on the ridge and their big guns were placed so that most of them could not be depressed sufficently to rake the Federals coming up from below. Also, the

In command of the Second Minnesota regiment at Missionary ridge was dashing Lt. Col. Judson W. Bishop, 32, of Chatfield.   Minnesota Historical Society

Confederates could see too much. Though veterans, they apparently were overawed by the sight of the Union strength forming on the plain and gave way when the attack was made. Regardless of poor Confederate leadership, however, the Cumberlanders had made amends for Chickamauga.

The Second Minnesota under Lt. Col. Judson W. Bishop "did itself proud" going up the ridge after its skirmishing role already described. The regiment had 185 men in the attack (150 more were on detached service) and was credited with capturing two 12-pound Napoleon guns at the top. It lost eight killed and 31 wounded at Missionary ridge. Six of seven members of its color guard fell.

One attacking Minnesotan—Capt. Jeremiah C. Donahower of company E, a St. Peter banker—described the climax of the assault thus: "The hill was steep and rifted, and the ascent was necessarily slow and retarded by the fire of the retiring Confederates, and from those behind the works above, but higher and still higher we moved toward those smoking cannon then almost within our grasp. At last the crest was reached, the log barricade crossed at a bound, and there in the arena of strife and confusion for a brief moment we stood—dazed by the scene."

Like most of the regiments, the Second Minnesota had its heroes. One was Sgt. Axel H. Reed of company K, a Glencoe farmer-bricklayer-trapper. He had broken arrest at Chickamauga to fight bravely there, and at Missionary ridge he led his company after its officers fell. Although he lost an arm, he declined discharge and remained on active duty to the end of the war.

Color Sgt. Holder Jacobus of company E "crossed lances" with a Confederate color bearer over one of the cannon the regiment captured. Then Jacobus fell wounded.

After Cpl. John Mullen of company D was wounded carrying the colors, Sgt. George W. Shuman of company I took them and (said Bishop) "kept them aloft and in front through the hottest of the fight."

After the battle a soldier in company H—Billings J. Sibley of Mankato—wrote his father that the Confederates "got pretty well paid for Chattanooga." The Federals had pierced the Confederate mountain defense line, upset the southern communication system by capturing Chattanooga and had left the gate open for Sherman to divide the Confederacy in two.

The Second Minnesota had won less hazardous service for itself the rest of the war. After playing a relatively minor role in the Atlanta campaign, the regiment marched to the sea and through the Carolinas with Sherman. It took part in the grand review of the Union armies in Washington May 24, 1865, and the following July 20 was discharged at Fort Snelling.

CAPTURE OF LITTLE ROCK

FOR THE THIRD MINNESOTA regiment, there was a marked contrast between two Julys during the Civil war.

In July 1862 the regiment suffered the great embarrassment of being surrendered to raiding Confederates at Murfreesboro, Tenn. (We'll return to that later.)

In July 1863, though, things were different. The Third Minnesota was part of the Union army t h a t besieged and captured the Confederate stronghold of Vicksburg, Miss. The prize included a Confederate army.

It was in July 1863, too, that the Third Minnesota was ordered to take a steamer from Vicksburg up the Mississippi river to Helena, Ark. There it became part of another victorious excursion into Rebel-held territory—Gen. Frederick Steele's little-known expedition to drive the Confederates out of Arkansas and occupy the capital, Little Rock, on the Arkansas river. Union capture of Vicksburg July 4 (and of Port Hudson, La., July 9) had opened the Mississippi and, among other things, cleared the way for a campaign against Confederates in Arkansas. Advisability of such a move had been underscored by an unsuccessful Rebel attempt to take Helena July 4 (the same day Vicksburg fell) and once again close off the Mississippi River to the north.

The Third Minnesota, about 400 strong, arrived at Helena July 26, 1863, and found the place so hot that the men put an arbor of tree branches over their tents. Steele took over command of "the army to take the field from Helena" on Aug. 5. The heat was still intense Aug. 13 when the Third Minnesota and the rest of Steele's army of about 7,000 men became "Arkansas travelers" by starting their march for Little Rock, some 100 miles to the west. The Arkansas capital was held by nearly 8,000 Confederates under able Gen. Sterling (Pap) Price of Missouri.

Leading the Minnesotans during the campaign was their newly named colonel, Christopher Columbus Andrews, a St. Cloud lawyer who later was promoted to brigadier general. After the war Andrews had a distinguished career as minister to Sweden and Norway, United States consul general in Brazil, and as Minnesota's "apostle of forestry" who strove mightily to save the state's tree resources.

Halfway to Little Rock—at DeVall's Bluff on the White river—Steele's force was joined by 6,000 cavalry under Gen. John W. Davidson. Addition of an infantry brigade a little later swelled Steele's army to some 14,500. Widespread sickness, however, shrank the effective force to about 10,500. "The sick list is frightful," Steele wrote during the stay at DeVall's Bluff. Although the Third Minnesota suffered less than most of

Here nattily dressed in his Civil war uniform, Christopher C. Andrews was the able colonel of the Third Minnesota during the Arkansas campaign. He was promoted to brigadier general and was brevetted major general. Minnesota Historical Society

the units, it reported 52 sick and 362 fit for duty on Aug. 31.

The army moved again toward Little Rock on Sept. 1 and the area it now traversed (but not the weather) reminded some Third regiment men of "the beautiful prairies of Minnesota."

Price had entrenched most of his Confederate troops—about 6,500 of them—north of the Arkansas river and disposed the rest on the south side with orders to prevent Union forces from crossing. With this placement of troops, Price obviously hoped Steele would attack from the north side. But Steele had the good sense to send Davidson and his cavalrymen across the Arkansas about 10 miles below Little Rock. This was done with very little opposition.

Then Steele's infantry, including the Third Minnesota, moved toward Confederate works on the north bank while Davidson's cavalry approached Little Rock on the south side. Seeing that this maneuver would turn his north-bank fortifications, Price on Sept. 10 withdrew his troops across the Arkansas, evacuated Little Rock about 5 p.m. and retreated to Arkadelphia to the southwest. The Confederates left so hurriedly they failed to destroy their pontoon bridge over the river at Little Rock.

Davidson took over the city the evening of the 10th and found the old United States arsenal there intact. The arsenal had been in Confederate hands since Feb. 8, 1861, when Arkansas authorities had seized it. Little Rock had fallen with very little bloodshed.

Of the Little Rock campaign, the late Kenneth P. Williams wrote in the fifth volume of "Lincoln Finds a General": "While some of Stonewall Jackson's moves have been praised until they are known to even a casual student of the war, the brilliance and boldness of Steele's performance in treacherous terrain and against an able and alerted enemy have attracted little attention."

Steele's infantry crossed the river the morning of Sept. 11. The Third Minnesota marched over the pontoon bridge and entered Little Rock about 7 a.m., as pictured in Stanley Arthurs' painting in the Minnesota state capitol. Andrews was riding up the high ground from the landing when Steele came over and informed the Minnesotans' colonel he was to be commander of Little Rock occupation forces. Steele added that the Third Minnesota would be part of the garrison "because of its efficiency and good discipline."

The Third Minnesota marched down the main street to the capitol and raised the United States flag on the dome. The flag remained there the rest of the war. The Minnesotans set up quarters near the capitol and frequently drilled on the capitol grounds during the nine months they remained on guard duty in Little Rock.

As post commander, Andrews headed a brigade composed of the 43rd Illinois regiment and Seventh Missouri cavalry besides the Third Minnesota. Given immediate command of the Minnesota regiment was Lt. Col. Hans Mattson, a Red Wing lawyer who had founded the Swedish settlement of Vasa in Goodhue county. He later became colonel of the regiment and after the war put out a number of Swedish publications. He was United States consul general in India from 1881 to 1883.

The Minnesotans and the rest of the garrison got along well with the Little Rock people (the city's population in 1860 was 3,727). There was a "respectable Union element" and in January 1864 the Third Minnesota saw formation of a free state government in Arkansas. Isaac Murphy was elected governor. For Murphy's inauguration the following April, the Third Minnesota marched "in a fine civic and military procession."

All the rest of the Third Minnesota's service was in Arkansas away from the main currents of war. The regiment was involved in a number of minor engagements. In one of these—the battle of Fitzhugh's Woods near Augusta, Ark.—it lost 7 killed and 16 wounded. The battle was a Union victory in which, says historian William W. Folwell, Col. Andrews "displayed tactical ability worthy of a much greater arena." The rest of the time the regiment battled disease, particularly malaria, rather than Confederates.

When the Third Minnesota was mustered out in September 1865, the men could look back with satisfaction over their two years of able service in "out-of-the-way" Arkansas. When the men looked back even further, however, they probably wished they could forget. To tell that story, we have to backtrack in time to July 1862 and travel to Murfreesboro, Tenn.

At that time the Third regiment, which had

been organized the previous November, was on guard duty at Murfreesboro as part of the 23rd brigade of the northern Army of the Ohio. Also stationed at Murfreesboro were six companies of the Ninth Michigan regiment, two small cavalry units and a battery—from 1,100 to 1,200 men in all. Temporarily in command of the entire garrison was Col. Henry C. Lester of the Third Minnesota. He had been a highly regarded captain with the First Minnesota in the east and was greatly admired as a fine officer by men of the Third Minnesota. But something happened to him at Murfreesboro.

Although Murfreesboro w a s an important transportation center, no defensive works had been put up. Also, Lester had made the error of dividing his forces. The Michigan regiment and cavalry encamped on a turnpike three-fourths of a mile east of town, while the Minnesotans and the battery encamped on the Nashville turnpike about a mile and a half northwest of Murfreesboro.

This was the situation July 13, 1862, when the garrison was surprised, to put it mildly, by a raiding force of 1,500 Confederates (maybe less) under notorious Gen. Nathan Bedford Forrest. This was the first of Forrest's many raids that soon made his name feared throughout the west.

Striking at daybreak, Forrest's raiders quickly captured the picket guard and the city. Then the Confederates attacked the Union camp east of Murfreesboro. The Michigan regiment put up a gallant defense but had to surrender about noon.

When he heard firing, Lester moved the Third Minnesota about half a mile eastward toward town. There the regiment took up a good defensive position but (Andrews later wrote in bitterness) "was kept standing or lying motionless hour after hour, even while plainly seeing the smoke rising from our burning depot of supplies." Andrews added that several officers begged Lester to go to the aid of the Michigan men but had to be satisfied with the reply, "We will see."

While Lester kept most of the regiment inactive near town, Forrest led a detachment of Confederates in an attack on the Minnesotans' camp, held by a band of 20 teamsters, convalescents and cooks under Cpl. Charles H. Green of Morrison county. The defense was so spirited, Forrest had to charge three times before taking the camp. Green died of wounds two hours later. The camp force, wrote historian Folwell, "showed how the men of the Third would have fought if they had had a commander of his (Green's) mettle."

Forrest was a cagey bluffer as well as stout fighter. The Federals at Murfreesboro had about as many men as he had, but Forrest used the time-honored stratagem of moving his men back and forth to give the impression his force was larger than it was. Also, Forrest "buffaloed" the Third Minnesota's colonel with a tough note: "I must demand an unconditional surrender of your forces as prisoners of war, or I will have every man put to the sword. You are aware of the overpowering force I have at my command, and this demand is made to prevent the further effusion of blood."

In the afternoon Lester conferred with the captured Michigan colonel (W. W. Duffield) in town and then called a council of Minnesota officers to consider surrender. The majority at first voted to fight, but Lester reopened the matter after some officers left. In the second vote, by ballot, six were for surrender and three for doing battle. Two of the latter, Chauncey W. Griggs and Andrews, later became colonels.

So the regiment was surrendered. The news, said Andrews, "was received by the men with sorrow and indignation too deep for utterance. They silently, though with tears in their eyes, gave up the well-kept arms which, through many months of hard service, they had honored."

Andrews also said the Confederates were astonished and delighted "at the capture they had so cheaply made." Not included in the surrender were 45 men of the Third regiment's company C. They were on detached service and later joined the Second Minnesota for a time.

The Third Minnesota's officers eventually were taken to Libby prison in Richmond, Va. They were later paroled. Lester and other officers who voted for surrender were dishonorably dismissed from the service Dec. 1, 1862. Non-commissioned officers and enlisted men of the regiment were paroled at McMinnville, Tenn. They were sent to St. Louis, Mo., and on Aug. 28, 1862, embarked from there to help quell the Sioux Indian uprising that had broken out in Minnesota 10 days before.

The Third regiment reached Fort Snelling Sept. 4. Nine days later it arrived at Fort Ridgely, on the Minnesota river upstream from New Ulm, to fight the Sioux as part of an expedition shaping up under Col. Henry H. Sibley, former governor. By this time the key battles of Fort Ridgely, New Ulm and Birch Coulee had been fought and the Indians under Little Crow had retreated to the Upper Agency area near the mouth of the Yellow Medicine river.

A former officer of the First Minnesota, Maj. Abraham E. Welch, now commanded the Third Minnesota. Sibley's force, which also included elements of the Sixth and Seventh regiments as well as other detachments, left Ridgely Sept. 19 to catch up with the Indians. After three days' march, Sibley's men encamped the night of Sept. 22 near a small lake a couple of miles from the Yellow Medicine river. Out ahead, Little Crow concealed his warriors—700 to 1,200 of them— in such a way that they could ambush the soldiers at daylight on Sept. 23.

Fortunately for Sibley and his force, the discipline of the Third Minnesota wasn't what it had been, or would be again when it returned to the south. Several men of the Third took it upon themselves to form a foraging party to go after some potatoes at the mouth of the Yellow Medicine. They piled into four or five wagons and at an early hour headed across the rolling prairie.

A short distance from camp they accidentally "sprang" the Sioux trap. Indians jumped up and fired, killing one Third Minnesota soldier and wounding others. The soldiers leaped to the ground and returned the fire. This episode triggered the so-called battle of Wood Lake, which was a decisive white victory and brought an end to organized Indian warfare in Minnesota. Although other troops fought well, the Third Minnesota bore the brunt of the battle—and the casualties. The regiment lost five killed and 27 wounded at Wood Lake.

The Third Minnesota proved to be a rallying outfit. From the "haymaker" at Murfreesboro it recovered to help defeat Indians in Minnesota and Confederates in Mississippi and Arkansas.

As part of the garrison at Little Rock, the Third Minnesota was photographed on dress parade in front of the Arkansas state capitol. The regiment was on guard duty at Little Rock about nine months, drilled on the capitol grounds.

Hans Mattson became colonel of the Third Minnesota in Arkansas after Andrews stepped up to a larger command. Like Andrews, he was a top-notch officer and had a prominent postwar career.

Minnesota Historical Society

The Third Minnesota moved from Vicksburg to Helena and over to Little Rock.

Map by Warner Nelson

VICTORY AT VICKSBURG

The Great C.S.A. is now severed in twain,
And both of them shortly must die;
But he will not forget till the end of his reign,
That wonderful Fourth of July!

Bring out the spare powder and fire the big guns,
The Rebs are surprised at the way
Columbia's loyal and true-hearted sons
Have honored the country's birthday.

From "Vicksburg Is Taken, Boys,"
by C. W. Hicks

HARD-BITTEN SOLDIERS of Gen. Ulysses S. Grant's Army of the Tennessee, including the Fourth Minnesota regiment, cheered and waved flags and shot off fireworks to celebrate the fall of Vicksburg, Miss., July 4, 1863. Down on the Mississippi river below, equally dogged sailors of Adm. David Dixon Porter's fleet fired guns with considerable gusto.

The Fourth Minnesota's brigade commander, Col. (later Gen.) John B. Sanborn, wrote that "there was a scene of life and joy and excitement

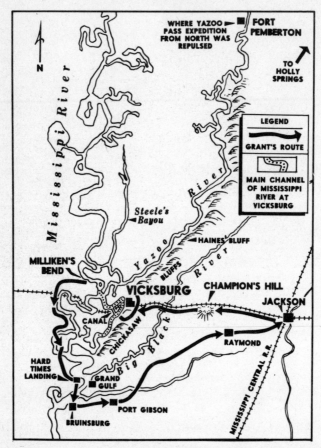

Minneapolis Tribune Picture Magazine Map

such as is rarely seen on this planet."

Nevertheless, considering the provocation, the Union men who captured Vicksburg observed their victory in an orderly manner. They might have been forgiven an unrestrained demonstration, because it had taken them seven months, including a six-week siege and one of the most admired military campaigns in history, to conquer the Confederacy's chief stronghold on the Mississippi river.

In the afternoon of July 3, about the same time that the repulse of Pickett's charge meant defeat of another southern army at Gettysburg, Pa., the Confederate commander at Vicksburg had sent a white flag through the lines and asked for surrender terms.

He was Gen. John C. Pemberton, a northerner who cast his lot with the south. Though brave and loyal to the Confederacy, he was not completely trusted by many southerners. Pemberton, whose prewar service had included a hitch on the Minnesota frontier, made plenty of mistakes in defense of Vicksburg, but he also was the victim of conflicting orders by superiors and had the bad luck to come up against Grant at his best.

Grant at first demanded "unconditional surrender," as he had earlier at Fort Donelson, Tenn. Pemberton wouldn't go for that, so Grant relented and let the more than 31,000 Confederate soldiers at Vicksburg give their paroles, stack their arms and go home. Besides the city and Pemberton's army, the Union "take" at Vicksburg included 172 cannon and 60,000 small arms.

The victory at Vicksburg, plus the capture of Port Hudson, La., a few days later, gave the north control of the Mississippi river all the way from Minnesota to the gulf. As Lincoln put it, "The Father of Waters again goes unvexed to the sea." The Confederacy, split in two, had been dealt a

Col. (later Gen.) John B. Sanborn of St. Paul commanded the brigade of which the Fourth Minnesota was part at Vicksburg.   Minnesota Historical Society

blow from which it never recovered. And Grant had earned a reputation that would lead him to over-all command of Union armies and to ultimate victory in the east.

In a postwar address published in "Glimpses of the Nation's Struggle" (Second Series), Sanborn said nearly all the officers of Grant's army had acquired new uniforms in anticipation of the surrender of Vicksburg. "On the morning of the July 4," said Sanborn, "all such uniforms were put on, every enlisted man burnished his gun so that it glimmered in the sunshine like pure silver, the bands of music took their position at a little after sunrise, and the commands marched from their camping-places . . . through the city to the courthouse and the banks of the Mississippi river."

The Fourth Minnesota regiment, which had been all through the Vicksburg campaign as part of Gen. James B. McPherson's 17th corps, claimed to be the first unit to march into the city July 4 and the first to plant its colors over the Warren county courthouse in Vicksburg. The 45th Illinois regiment, part of Gen. John A. Logan's division of the 17th corps, claimed the same honor. Says Edwin C. Bearss, present research historian of Vicksburg national military park: "Undoubtedly, the colors of both the 45th Illinois and the Fourth Minnesota were raised over the courthouse on July 4. The question of which was raised first is one that is open to controversy."

There was no doubt about the matter as far as Sanborn was concerned. (A St. Paulite who had served as Gov. Alexander Ramsey's adjutant general, Sanborn was colonel of the Fourth Minnesota when it first went south in April 1862. During the Vicksburg campaign he commanded the Fourth Minnesota's brigade—the first brigade of the seventh division of the 17th corps—and part of the time even headed the division when its regular commander, Gen. Isaac F. Quinby, was sick. Immediate command of the Fourth Minnesota went to Lt. Col. John E. Tourtellotte of Mankato. He later became colonel and headed the regiment in an able manner for the rest of

71

the war.)

Sanborn said McPherson came to him "in person" the evening of July 3 and indicated that Sanborn's brigade and one from Logan's division "were designated to take possession of Vicksburg and take charge of guarding and paroling the prisoners, for the reason that they had fought the hardest and suffered the most in the campaign." Then Sanborn stated explicitly: "As ordered by Gen. McPherson I led the column that marched into Vicksburg, and the Fourth Minnesota band and regiment led my brigade." The painting in the Minnesota state capitol shows Sanborn riding into Vicksburg at the head of his troops.

The "first troops in Vicksburg" question, although of no great moment, is one of many unresolved controversies adding fascination to the study of the Civil war.

The Fourth Minnesota's historian, Alonzo L. Brown of Sumter (later of Brownton), wrote that he and another soldier walked into the city apart from the others "and concluded they would be among the first ones in, as no person was ahead." He added: "We walked to the courthouse at a lively pace . . . [It] was about two and a half miles from our line and had been a common target for the Union artillerists and could be plainly seen from most of the line. Hundreds of shots were fired at it, but the only one that struck it that we could discover was on the side of one of the four columns of the cupola, which had a piece cut out of its side."

Musician George E. Sly of Belle Plaine, who

This granite obelisk honors Minnesota troops who fought at Vicksburg. Dedicated in 1907, it features a bronze statue of peace at the base.

Ryland M. Rudd — Vicksburg National Military Park

served in the Fourth regiment's company A, recorded the time in his diary: "At 4 p.m. we marched into the city and stacked arms at the courthouse. Had half an hour to look around and then marched back to camp."

John H. Thurston of Lakeville and company C was enthusiastic: "I have just been up on the hill and saw the rebels marching out and stacking their arms. Our forces are also moving in. Marched into Vicksburg, banners flying and music playing. This is the most glorious Fourth of July I ever spent. Fireworks seem to be all around the lines."

Like the Fourth Minnesota, the Fifth Minnesota regiment, under Col. Lucius F. Hubbard (a future governor), was in on most of the Vicksburg campaign. When the city fell, the Fifth Minnesota was on detached service across the river in Louisiana. Most of the regiment took a little steamer over the Mississippi and landed at the Vicksburg wharf July 4 to help celebrate.

In addition to the Fourth and Fifth regiments, Minnesota had two other units at Vicksburg at the time of the surrender and presumably they also enjoyed the occasion. They were the First battery of light artillery, which helped besiege the city, and the Third Minnesota regiment, which was part of the reinforcements that arrived June 8. Stationed on bluffs northeast of Vicksburg, the Third regiment helped discourage another army from coming to Pemberton's relief.

The Fourth Minnesota moved into Vicksburg as part of the occupation force and helped guard prisoners until their parole was completed. During this time the Minnesotans visited caves in which the populace had lived during the siege. Alonzo Brown wrote that the caves "seemed quite secure and comfortable. . . We expected to find that the shot and shell from our batteries and mortar fleet had caused great destruction of property, but to our astonishment we saw that . . . little damage had been done."

Late in July the regiment was made part of the provost guard in Vicksburg and kept to that duty the rest of the summer. Sickness greatly reduced the regiment's ranks. The men blamed the climate and the hard service they had endured during the Vicksburg campaign—which we'll now take up.

By the late spring of 1862, the capture of such Confederate river strongholds as Island No. 10, Memphis, Tenn., Fort Pillow, Tenn., and New Orleans, La., had left only a 250-mile stretch of the Mississippi from Vicksburg to Port Hudson in southern hands.

But Vicksburg was a Gibraltar with formidable defenses, both natural and man-made. It defied approach from almost any direction, especially the west and north. The city, which had a population of about 4,500 when war broke out, commanded a great hairpin curve in the Mississippi from 200-foot-high bluffs that extended along the east bank and trailed northeastward to the Yazoo river. Confederates fortified the area with numerous gun batteries not only at the city itself but above and below it (Grand Gulf, about 25 miles downstream, was a Confederate stronghold). No frontal attack from the west had a chance of success.

To the north a vast tangle of bayous, streams, swamps and flooded forests between the Yazoo and Mississippi river presented an almost impassable obstacle to invasion by a large army. Grant's forces would find that out the hard way.

If Grant's men could somehow get east of the city they might approach it from the "back door." But even there the way was rough because the bluffs behind Vicksburg were eroded into a network of ravines and steep-sided hills—natural bulwarks made stronger by Confederate fortifications.

Before hitting upon the plan of attack that finally succeeded, Grant tried several approaches that failed. His first fiasco was a combined land and water movement in December 1862. In northern Mississippi, Grant led some 40,000 men, including the Fourth and Fifth Minnesota regiments, south along the Mississippi Central railroad, hoping to attack Pemberton's forces from the rear. At the same time, Gen. William T. Sherman came down by boat with 30,000 men to assault Vicksburg from the water.

Grant had to give up his march, however, after Confederate cavalrymen disrupted his supply line and wrecked his supply base at Holly Springs, Miss., Dec. 20. Sherman, thus without land support, attacked Chickasaw Bluffs north of Vicksburg Dec. 27-29 and was repulsed.

In January 1863 Grant came down the river

to take command of Vicksburg maneuvers and set up headquarters at Milliken's Bend, La., on the west side of the river some 10 miles upstream from Vicksburg. Like the Yazoo delta to the north, the Louisiana side opposite Vicksburg was low, swampy and decidedly uncomfortable for troops.

At least three attempts to set up a water route that would bypass Vicksburg kept many of Grant's soldiers busy digging canals in the Louisiana "goo" during the winter. None of the schemes worked. Men of the Fifth Minnesota were among troops who dug. Col. Hubbard wrote afterward: "Standing in the water up to one's knees and delving in the mud with a spade was to their minds unsoldierly in the extreme and a mighty poor way to crush the rebellion."

Grant's forces also made two tries at crossing the Yazoo delta in an effort to turn the Confederate right at Vicksburg. Both of these strange expeditions were turned back. The Fourth Minnesota went along on the first—the so-called Yazoo Pass expedition—in March. After blasting a hole in the levee 325 miles north of Vicksburg, the troops rode navy transports through a sailor's nightmare of narrow, twisting waterways. Confederates felled trees to make the route more hazardous and then halted the invasion at Fort Pemberton, 100 miles or so north of Vicksburg. After returning to the Mississippi, the Minnesotans and the rest felt lucky to escape capture.

In a second expedition, this time up Steele's bayou, Adm. David D. Porter almost lost a fleet of 11 vessels before getting them out of a snarl of trees, water and mud.

At last, in April, Grant devised and put in motion a bold plan that historian Bruce Catton calls "the crucial Federal military decision of the war." The campaign thus launched not only brought about Vicksburg's capture but, in both conception and execution, is widely considered one of the greatest campaigns in military annals.

The problem was to get across the river below Vicksburg, where there was solid ground for fighting, and then to attack the fortress from the east. In the wet camps across the river from Vicksburg Grant had more than 40,000 men in three army corps: the 17th (including the Fourth Minnesota) under Gen. James B. McPherson; the 15th (including the Fifth Minnesota) under Gen. William T. Sherman, and the 13th under Gen. John A. McClernand, an Illinois politician

This lithograph shows the position of the Fourth Minnesota regiment and other units in its division during the siege of Vicksburg. Confederate forts crown the ridge in background. Two small trees at right and above center show where Pemberton talked surrender with Grant.

U.S. Signal Corps Photo in National Archives

who had hoped to be leading all the forces attacking Vicksburg but had to settle for less.

In April Grant had his men march 50 or 60 waterlogged miles down the Louisiana side to Hard Times Landing. "A worse march no army ever made," said the Fourth Minnesota's Col. John B. Sanborn.

Adm. Porter, at Grant's request, ran the Vicksburg batteries with gunboats and transports at midnight April 16. Losing only one transport, Porter brought Grant supplies and took his army across the river. Grant landed at Bruinsburg, Miss., 32 miles south of Vicksburg, with 33,000 men April 30, flanked the strong defenses at Grand Gulf and defeated Confederates who tried to stop him at Port Gibson.

Pemberton offered weak resistance partly because Grant had taken the trouble to confuse him. Sherman was left to make a diversion north of Vicksburg, after which his force (including the Fifth Minnesota) hurriedly caught up with the rest of the army by marching down the Louisiana side and crossing the river. Also, an Illinois music teacher who hated horses, Col. Benjamin H. Grierson, made a 600-mile cavalry raid across the state of Mississippi to Baton Rouge, La., to add to Pemberton's perplexity.

Once across the river, Grant took a great gamble that defied military convention. Perhaps remembering what happened to him at Holly Springs, Grant cut his army off from a supply base and decided to live off the country. His army, now numbering about 44,000, moved swiftly in three columns toward the Mississippi capital, Jackson, about 50 miles east of Vicksburg. Jackson was a key city on Vicksburg's supply route and also the place where Gen. Joseph E. Johnston was forming a relief army. Striking before Johnston was ready, Grant captured Jackson May 14 after a skirmish with Confederates at nearby Raymond two days earlier. Johnston retreated to the north.

Though he had less men at this time than Pemberton and Johnston combined, Grant had succeeded in putting his army between the Confederate forces with an excellent chance to take care of them individually.

Now Grant turned westward toward Vicksburg and Pemberton's army. Johnston had ordered Pemberton to come out of the city and strike the Union army from behind, but President Jefferson Davis told Pemberton to defend Vicksburg. Attempting to do a little of both, poor Pemberton groped for Grant's supply line but couldn't find any. He then decided to try to join Johnston but was too late. Grant brought Pemberton to battle at Champion's Hill, halfway between Vicksburg and Jackson, May 16 and defeated him in the decisive encounter of the campaign. The Fourth Minnesota was actively engaged at Champion's Hill and claimed the capture of 118 prisoners there.

The retreating Pemberton got his army back into the redoubts, lunettes and other fortifications ringing Vicksburg. Grant's army invested the citadel with a parallel ring, Sherman's corps taking position on the right, McPherson's in the center and McClernand's on the left.

Grant guessed, wrongly, that the Confederates had no more stomach for fighting. He ordered his men to storm the Rebel ramparts May 19 and again on May 22. Both assaults were hurled back with heavy losses—900 the first time, 3,200 the second.

In the May 22 onslaught the Fifth Minnesota escaped with only two killed and one wounded, but the Fourth Minnesota suffered 12 men killed and 42 wounded as it moved with the rest of Sanborn's brigade to an exposed position in support of McClernand's troops to the left. The Fourth would have had few casualties if McClernand had not given Grant the false impression he could win the day if Grant would send reinforcements and renew attacks elsewhere.

The Fourth Minnesota was part of the troops that Grant had McPherson send McClernand late in the day to try for a breakthrough. The Fourth moved in against the Second Texas lunette and then was astounded to see McClernand's troops there pull out, apparently under the impression they were being relieved. The result was slaughter of Sanborn's brigade. When darkness halted fighting, the Minnesotans hauled off an abandoned cannon but had to leave some of their dead and wounded on the field. The wounded suffered horribly for three days near the enemy's works before they and the dead were removed during a truce.

Grant now settled down to siege warfare. With re-establishment of a river supply line, his army was reinforced until it numbered 75,000 men. Except for a brief excursion to the north, the Fourth Minnesota joined the rest of the army in pushing trenches closer and closer to Vicksburg. There were numerous casualties every day, and also many instances of fraternizing, as the lines of the besiegers and besieged got to be only a few feet apart. It took about 45 days of "constriction" before the Confederates gave up, as already described.

The Fourth Minnesota stayed at Vicksburg until Sept. 12, 1863, when it was sent east to Chattanooga, Tenn. On Oct. 5, 1864, the regiment lost another 13 killed and 31 wounded when

Lt. Col. John E. Tourtellotte of Mankato had immediate command of the Fourth Minnesota at Vicksburg. He later became colonel.   Minnesota Historical Society

it helped repulse a Confederate attack on the Federal supply base at Allatoona, Ga. Lt. Col. John E. Tourtellotte of the regiment was the garrison commander. The battle is best remembered for having inspired evangelist Philip P. Bliss to write the hymn, "Hold the Fort."

Like the Second Minnesota, the Fourth Minnesota ended its service by marching with Sherman to the sea and in the grand review May 24, 1865, in Washington.

Grant's army dug canals in the Louisiana lowlands across the river from Vicksburg during the early months of 1863 in an effort to bypass the Confederate fortress. Below, the men are shown excavating a channel across the neck of the peninsula opposite Vicksburg.

None of the canals worked. Grant apparently didn't expect them to, but digging kept the soldiers busy during the winter. Col. Lucius F. Hubbard of the Fifth Minnesota said his men considered canal digging "the most menial" and "the most unprofitable" service they were called on to perform during the war.

Another kind of digging paid off later on—construction of zigzag trenches (saps) closer and closer to the Confederate works during Union siege operations in May and June 1863.

Above, is a Harper's Weekly drawing of sap operations in the area occupied by Gen. James B. McPherson's 17th corps, which included the Fourth Minnesota regiment.

Sap rollers (cylindrical objects of basketwork), shown beyond the soldiers in foreground, were unwound ahead of sappers (men constructing trenches) in order to provide cover against enemy snipers.

CRISIS AT CORINTH

HE CHAPLAIN PRAISED the Lord and passed the ammunition. The colonel, usually quiet and dignified in camp, urged his men on by shouting and waving his sword from his prancing steed. And six companies of the Fifth Minnesota regiment, lately in need of discipline but now drilled into an efficient outfit, struck hard at the flank of Confederates who were pouring through a gap in the Union line. The southerners were stopped. They soon retreated and before long the battle was over.

The chaplain was the Rev. John Ireland, a newly ordained Roman Catholic priest who later would become a great archbishop of St. Paul. The colonel was Lucius F. Hubbard, a Red Wing newspaper editor-publisher who would serve as Minnesota's ninth governor from 1882 to 1887. The time of the battle was Oct. 4, 1862, in the second year of the Civil war. The scene was Corinth, Miss.

Corinth, in northeastern Mississippi just below the Tennessee line, was a transportation center of considerable strategic importance. The Confederacy's main east-west rail artery—the Memphis

& Charleston, linking the Mississippi valley with the east coast—crossed the north-south line of the Mobile & Ohio at Corinth. The junction was called Cross City when founded in 1855, but two years later the name was changed to Corinth after the ancient Greek crossroads city.

Besides controlling troop and supply movements by rail in four directions, Corinth was near such Tennessee river ports as Eastport, Miss., Pittsburg Landing, Tenn., and Hamburg, Tenn. Even when water was low, steamers could land at these places with freight and men, which then could be moved across country to Corinth.

The significance of Corinth as a military objective increased after Union forces under Gen. Ulysses S. Grant captured Forts Henry and Donelson in Tennessee in February 1862. The Confederate commander in the west, Gen. Albert Sidney Johnston, had to withdraw his troops from Kentucky and most of Tennessee. He formed a new defense line along the Memphis & Charleston railroad and by the end of March concentrated more than 40,000 men at Corinth. Second in command of Confederate forces at Corinth was Gen. P. G. T. Beauregard—a transfer from the east, where he had won fame at Fort Sumter and Bull Run.

Meanwhile, some 40,000 men of Grant's army moved south up the Tennessee river to Pittsburg Landing, 22 miles northeast of Corinth, and encamped near Shiloh church a short distance away. They had orders to wait for Gen. Don Carlos Buell and another Union army of 20,000 to join

The Rev. John Ireland is shown in 1862 when he was chaplain of the Fifth Minnesota. He became famed archbishop of St. Paul in 1888.

them from Nashville, Tenn. The combined armies then would go after the Confederates at Corinth.

Johnston decided to strike before the Union armies could unite. On April 3 about 40,000 Confederates marched north from Corinth and the morning of April 6 surprised the unentrenched Federals at their Shiloh camp. In several hours of confused, bloody fighting between two green armies, the Confederates nearly succeeded in driving the Union troops into the Tennessee river. That they didn't was due in large measure to Gen. Benjamin Prentiss' stand in the Hornets' Nest with troops that included the First Minnesota battery of light artillery. Although a monument now honors it at Shiloh, the battery never got sufficient recognition for its hard-nosed fighting there. It was Minnesota's only unit in the battle. The

Second Minnesota regiment arrived right after.

Grant himself reached the battlefield late and helped rally his men. The Confederate commander, Johnston, died from loss of blood from a leg wound and Beauregard took over. Most of Buell's reinforcing army joined Grant's during the night. The now-larger Union force pushed the Confederates back April 7. Beauregard ordered his defeated army to return to the defenses of Corinth. The killed and wounded in the terrible two days at Shiloh added up to nearly 25 per cent of the approximately 100,000 engaged.

For three weeks after the battle, Union forces stayed in camp around Shiloh to prepare for another advance on Corinth. Grant's superior at St. Louis, Mo., Gen. Henry W. (Old Brains) Halleck arrived to take charge and Grant was made second-in-command.

As Halleck began inching his way toward Corinth late in April, he had not only Grant's Army of the Tennessee and Buell's Army of the Ohio but also Gen. John Pope's Army of the Mississippi (fresh from victory at Island No. 10) —more than 90,000 men in all. Reinforcements soon swelled the total to 110,000. Unhappy that Grant's men had not been entrenched at Shiloh, the cautious Halleck insisted on having his huge army dig in at the end of every day's march. The result was that Halleck took about a month to cover the 20 miles to Corinth's outer defenses.

The Fourth Minnesota regiment under Col. John B. Sanborn went south for the first time in April. It arrived before Corinth May 15 and became part of Pope's Army of the Mississippi that was helping invest the town.

A few days later, on May 24, the newly organized Fifth Minnesota regiment, minus companies B, C and D that were detached to garrison frontier forts at home, also joined Pope's force near Corinth. Colonel of the Fifth Minnesota at that time was Rudolph von Borgersrode, who had seen service in the Prussian army. The Fifth was assigned to Gen. David S. Stanley's division and to a brigade (eventually commanded by Col. Joseph A. Mower) that included the Eighth Wisconsin regiment. The latter's mascot was a bald eagle, Old Abe, that had "joined up" at Eau Claire. Old Abe became so famous the Eighth Wisconsin was called the Eagle regiment and the entire brigade at length was known as the Eagle brigade.

On May 28, only four days after reaching the front, the Fifth Minnesota lost three killed and 12 wounded in an engagement at Farmington, Miss., near Corinth.

Although he had built up a force of about 65,000 at Corinth, Beauregard felt he was no match for the Federals closing in on him. The night of May 29-30, 1862, he gave Halleck the slip and retreated to the south. The Federals moved into Corinth unopposed May 30. Thus ended the *siege* of Corinth which often is confused with the *battle* of Corinth that took place the following Oct. 3-4, was mentioned at the start of this chapter and will be dealt with later. Through no fault of the men in the ranks, Hal-

In this tintype, Col. (later Gen.) Lucius F. Hubbard (seated, left) is pictured with other officers of the Fifth Minnesota: Lt. Col. William B. Gere (seated, right), Adj. Thomas P. Gere (standing, left) and Lt. William B. McGrorty, quartermaster. The latter drowned crossing the Mississippi river ice at La Crosse, Wis., near the end of the war. Thomas Gere joined the regiment after fighting at Fort Ridgely, Minn., during the Sioux Uprising of 1862.

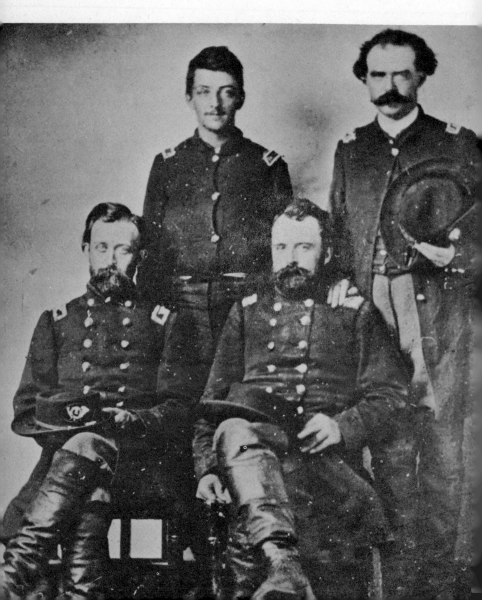

leck's "horde" had taken too long to capture Corinth. Nevertheless the Union army had cut the vital east-west railroad and now could establish its own line there.

During the summer of 1862 the Fifth Minnesota did picket duty east of Corinth along the Memphis & Charleston and helped "occupy the country." While stationed at Camp Clear Creek, Miss., the regiment suffered greatly from typhoid, malaria and kindred diseases.

Father Ireland, who succeeded the Rev. James F. Chaffee as the regiment's chaplain in June, worked hard to bring comfort to the men during the "sickly" summer campaign. A large, robust, jovial man of 24, Ireland had been ordained a priest in St. Paul the previous December after studying in France. For Ireland's first sermon in the field under the hot Mississippi sun, men of the Fifth regiment built him an altar, pulpit and canopy of saplings and leaves. They also gave up their games of chuck-a-luck to listen to what the new chaplain had to say. Ireland himself was a chess enthusiast and after supper at night frequently played chess with the soldiers.

Ireland was popular with men of all faiths not only in the Fifth Minnesota but in the entire brigade. In 1910, by which time he had been archbishop 22 years, Ireland received a birthday greeting from the Rev. Robert J. Burdette of Los Angeles' Temple Baptist church, who in 1862 had been a private in the 47th Illinois regiment, part of the Fifth Minnesota's brigade. Burdette reminded the archbishop that "the entire brigade called you its chaplain and time and promotion have not moved you from the place you then held in a soldier's heart." Ireland remained chaplain until April 1863, when ill health during the Vicksburg campaign forced him to resign.

Conditions improved for men of the Fifth Minnesota when in August 1862 their camp was moved to a "more favorable" site near Tuscumbia, Ala. At Tuscumbia, Col. Borgersrode resigned and Lt. Col. Lucius F. Hubbard, 26, became colonel of the regiment. Maj. William B. Gere of Chatfield was promoted to lieutenant colonel. According to the Eagle brigade commander, Col. Joseph A. Mower, Hubbard found the Fifth Minnesota "in a low state of discipline, but by strict attention to his duties . . . made it one of the most efficient regiments in this brigade."

Hubbard had founded the Red Wing Republican, forerunner of the present Daily Republican Eagle, in 1857. He had enlisted as a private in company A of the Fifth Minnesota Dec. 19, 1861, and quickly worked his way up. Although without previous military experience, he was an able, efficient officer respected by his men.

Another interesting recruit in company A was John Arkins of Red Wing, who worked on Hubbard's paper. Whenever he could, Arkins read from a volume of William Shakespeare's plays that he carried with him in the field. Long after the war, Arkins became one of the best known newspapermen in the west as manager of the Rocky Mountain News at Denver, Colo.

The Fifth Minnesota's brigade was called the Eagle brigade after Old Abe, eagle mascot of the Eighth Wisconsin regiment. The bird is perched on his standard (above) with Wisconsin soldiers in the field during southern service.

While the Fifth Minnesota spent a relatively quiet summer, there were several troop and command shifts that would affect the regiment.

After capturing Corinth, Halleck divided up his huge force and then moved to Washington as general in chief of the Union armies, leaving Grant in charge of 50,000 men or less with which to hold western Tennessee and northern Mississippi. Gen. John Pope went east to command the new Union Army of Virginia and Gen. William S. Rosecrans succeeded him as head of Grant's left wing, the Army of the Mississippi, which included both the Fourth and Fifth Minnesota regiments. Gen. Don Carlos Buell, reinforced with troops that had fought at Shiloh, moved toward Chattanooga, Tenn., but got caught up in a race for Louisville, Ky., and the Ohio river with Beauregard's successor, Confederate Gen. Braxton Bragg.

The jig appeared to be up for the Confederacy in May 1862 when Corinth fell in the west and Gen. George B. McClellan's Peninsular campaign appeared about to end in the capture of Richmond, Va., in the east.

But during the summer southern prospects brightened considerably. McClellan failed to take Richmond and retreated, after which Gen. Robert E. Lee's Army of Northern Virginia defeated Pope's army at Second Bull Run and then, in September, invaded Maryland.

Also in September, Bragg invaded Kentucky and had the Union's Buell, among many others, worried he would reach the Ohio river. The same month, too, Grant's depleted forces looked like an inviting target to two Confederate commanders in the west—Generals Earl Van Dorn and Sterling Price—and they decided to combine and strike Rosecrans' divisions of Grant's army in the Corinth area (Grant himself was stationed at Jackson, Tenn.)

Gettysburg has been called "the high tide of

the Confederacy," but, as several historians have pointed out, the real "high tide" was in September 1862 when southern armies were advancing on three widely separated fronts.

Soon, however, the fortunes of war turned once more against the Confederacy. Lee's invasion of the north was thwarted by McClellan in the decisive battle of Antietam (Sharpsburg), Md., Sept. 17 and the Confederates retreated to Virginia. Buell stopped Bragg's invasion of Kentucky at Perryville Oct. 8. And on Oct. 3-4, 1862, Rosecrans turned back Van Dorn and Price at Corinth.

In a preliminary to the battle of Corinth, Rosecrans attacked Price Sept. 19 at Iuka, Miss., 20 miles to the southeast. Price escaped to the southwest and joined Van Dorn at Ripley, Miss. The Fourth Minnesota lost three killed and 44 wounded at Iuka; the Fifth Minnesota was held in reserve there.

Van Dorn, the senior Confederate commander, and Price had 22,000 troops. Rosecrans had 15,000 men at Corinth and 8,000 more in towns nearby. Van Dorn determined to strike Rosecrans before he could collect all his men together. The Confederates moved northward, made a feint at Bolivar, Tenn., and then turned sharply to the east along the Memphis & Charleston and attacked Rosecrans Oct. 3. Before the first day of the battle was over, the southerners drove the Federals from Corinth's outer defenses (erected months before by the Confederates themselves) into an inner line right by the town. The Fourth Minnesota regiment and the First Minnesota battery got into the battle that day but the Fifth Minnesota was detached to guard a bridge over the Tuscumbia river southwest of Corinth.

The Fifth Minnesota still guarded the bridge and apparently was forgotten the evening of Oct. 3 w h i l e Rosecrans and his staff feverishly strengthened the Corinth lines for another day's battle. However, Lt. William B. McGrorty of St. Paul, whose duties as quartermaster included keeping Col. Hubbard's "cupboard" full, was in town for provisions and he reminded Rosecrans of the regiment's whereabouts. McGrorty was ordered to tell Hubbard to move the regiment into town and he did so.

The Fifth regiment made a dangerous march after dark and bivouacked near the Mobile & Ohio tracks on the northwest edge of town. The regiment was rudely awakened early Oct. 4 when an enemy shell landed close by.

Starting about 10 a.m., Oct. 4, the Confederates launched two attacks (fortunately for the Federals not very well co-ordinated) from woods north and northwest of Corinth. These assaults were repulsed in two hours or so of intense, bloody fighting in 94-degree heat.

The more publicized attack was aimed at the Union stronghold, battery Robinett, and ended when brave Col. William P. Rogers of the Second Texas regiment died, colors in hand, at the foot of the parapets. Men in Robinett had held.

The other attack, to the northwest, almost succeeded—and might have but for six companies of the Fifth Minnesota (one company was de-

tached on skirmish duty and three others were
still on the Minnesota frontier). Stationed in reserve next to a public square inside the town,
the Fifth Minnesota saw a large force of Price's
Confederates pour through a gap in the Union
lines to the right and head for an artillery park
in the square. The Eighth Wisconsin's eagle is
said to have screamed at the invaders.

Gen. Stanley, commander of the Fifth Minnesota's division, had ordered Hubbard to go to
the right to support a battery. But the battery had
disappeared. Anticipating orders, Hubbard had
his men face the attacking Confederates and fire
several volleys into them. When ammunition got
low, Father Ireland hurried to the rear with haver-
sacks and returned with cartridges for the men.
At the proper moment, Hubbard waved his sword
from his horse and led his men in a charge on the

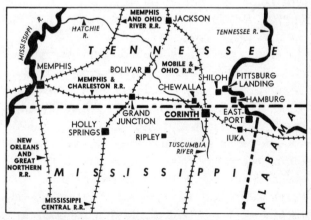

Minneapolis Tribune Picture Magazine Map

bewildered Confederates, as pictured in the state capitol painting. Other regiments joined the Minnesotans and the southerners beat a hasty retreat out of the town and back to the woods from which they had started their attack. Shortly after, the battle ended. Confederates retreated just as Federal reinforcements arrived. Ever after the Fifth regiment felt it had saved the day at Corinth.

Both Rosecrans and Stanley mentioned the Fifth Minnesota's charge in their official reports. Stanley said he was "happy to bear testimony to the gallant fight of this little regiment, commanded by Col. Hubbard. Few regiments on the field did more effective killing than they."

Chaplain Ireland wrote right after the battle: "I am proud of the Fifth regiment, and every one here feels proud of it. Great is our renown in this army." On Oct. 13, the colonel wrote his Aunt Mary Hubbard of Chester, Vt.: "I am proud to say that my regiment bore a most distinguished and important part in the fight and contributed largely in achieving the glorious results of our great victory."

Corinth was one of the most fiercely contested "small" battles of the war. Federal losses were about 2,500 and Confederate losses have been variously estimated from 4,200 to 4,800 killed, wounded or missing. These figures include losses suffered in an engagement near the Hatchie river during the rather futile Federal pursuit.

The Fifth regiment's casualties at Corinth were seven killed and 16 wounded. The Fourth regiment's were two killed and 10 wounded as it fought on the extreme right of the Union line.

Corinth helped point the way to the fall of Vicksburg, Miss., some nine months later. Both the Fourth and Fifth Minnesota regiments became part of Grant's Army of the Tennessee after Corinth and helped capture Vicksburg.

HE ONLY TIME Union troops all but annihilated a Confederate army on the field of battle during the Civil war was at Nashville, Tenn., Dec. 15-16, 1864.

In two days of maneuvering, attacking and shooting just south of the Tennessee capital, some 55,000 Federals under Gen. George H. (Rock of Chickamauga) Thomas routed 25,000 or less Confederates commanded by Gen. John B. Hood. Occurring at a time when Union armies in the east under Gen. Ulysses S. Grant were tightening a squeeze on Gen. Robert E. Lee's embattled defenders of Richmond, Va., the battle of Nashville did much to hasten the end of the war four months later.

Whether or not Nashville was *"the* decisive battle of the war," as its outstanding historian maintains, it certainly was *a* decisive battle. And right in the thick of the culminating attack and breakthrough that brought the smashing Union victory at Nashville were four Minnesota regiments—the Fifth, Seventh, Ninth and 10th. Together they made up the largest contingent to represent the state in a major Civil war battle.

Their total casualties—302 killed, wounded or missing—also were the greatest Minnesota suffered in any engagement of the war. Gen. Thomas reported his casualties for the two days at only 3,061, so the Minnesota loss was 10 per cent of the Union total—this in spite of the fact Minnesota troops numbered considerably less than 10 per cent of the Federal force.

Hood's defeat, as historian Stanley Horn of Nashville has pointed out, finally turned the south's left flank (military parlance, in the broadest sense, for the Confederate west). That's what Union forces in the west had been trying to do for three years or more. Northern victories at such places as Corinth and Vicksburg, Miss., (already covered in this book) had helped make the Nashville result possible by whittling down the Confederate left and weakening it, but the left flank was not shattered until Thomas licked Hood.

In a narrower sense, the battle of Nashville climaxed a series of military movements that had taken place during Hood's six-month tenure at the head of the south's able but ill-starred Army of Tennessee. Hood had assumed command of the army the previous July 17 when a struggle for Atlanta, Ga., was imminent between the Confederates and a much larger Union force under Gen. William T. Sherman.

Hood's predecessor, Gen. Joseph E. Johnston, had exasperated President Jefferson Davis by following a "back-up," Fabian policy. When he took over from Johnston, Hood understood that he was to do battle with Sherman. A large, combative

man with sad eyes, Hood, 33, had proved a hard
hitter in lesser commands. He had lost use of an
arm at Gettysburg and had had a leg amputated
after Chickamauga.

Unfortunately for the south, Hood lacked judg-
ment and other qualities necessary to be a good
army commander. At Atlanta, however, Hood did
what was expected of him when he gave it "the
old college try." Sherman's 100,000 men repulsed
Hood's determined attacks around Atlanta and
inflicted heavy casualties the Confederates could
ill afford. Sherman lost heavily, too, but casualties
were less damaging to him.

Sherman kept closing in and on Sept. 1, 1864,
Hood evacuated Atlanta. The Federals took over
the city the next day and made it their base of
operations. Hood retreated to figure out what to
do next.

During the summer the feared Confederate
cavalry raider, Gen. Nathan B. Forrest, had
wreaked havoc with Union communications in
Tennessee and elsewhere. Hood decided he too
could hamper Sherman—and maybe get him out
of Atlanta—by slashing at the Federal commander's long supply line between Chattanooga, Tenn.,
and Atlanta. Swinging north in late September,
Hood struck at Federal garrisons along the railroad coming down from Chattanooga.

The Fourth Minnesota, which had moved east
from Vicksburg, formed part of the garrison at
one of the railroad stations at Allatoona pass
northwest of Atlanta. On Oct. 5 the Fourth
helped beat off an attack by Hood's men and

thereby "held the fort."

Hood became such a serious threat that Sherman left a corps in Atlanta and took after the Confederate commander. Then followed t w o weeks or so of sparring and maneuvers, after which a strange situation developed. Both Sherman and Hood concocted bold plans that soon had the rival armies turning their backs on each other and heading in opposite directions to penetrate enemy territory.

Sherman decided to forget about a supply line, burn Atlanta and "make Georgia howl" by cutting a wide swath to the sea at Savannah, Ga. Earlier, Sherman had sent Gen. George H. Thomas, his capable but methodical lieutenant, to Nashville. There Thomas was to build up a force to act as a buffer against Forrest, Hood or any other possible invader. Before Ulysses S. Grant, general in chief of the armies, would approve of the plan, Sherman had to send two corps to reinforce Thomas. Then, on Nov. 15, Sherman started off with 60,000 men on his famed march to the sea.

Meanwhile Hood settled on a gamble that, considering the size of his army (less than 40,-000), was as daring as it was desperate. From northern Alabama Hood would cross the Tennessee river and defeat Thomas at Nashville. Then he might advance to the Ohio river and threaten Louisville, Ky., and Cincinnati, Ohio. He might even go east and help Lee. It was indeed a grandiose plan.

Hood's Tennessee campaign got a slow start

because of rains and supply difficulties. Although his army reached Florence, Ala., late in October, it didn't get across the Tennessee river until Nov. 16. Forrest's cavalry joined Hood and by Nov. 20 the Confederates were moving on Nashville by way of Spring Hill and Franklin, Tenn. Hood's delays had given Thomas some of the time he needed to concentrate forces at Nashville.

To delay Hood even longer, Thomas had Gen. John M. Schofield move south with his 23rd corps and the fourth corps under Gen. David S. Stanley. Schofield let Hood get between him and Nashville, however, and might well have been cut off and defeated at Spring Hill. But somehow Hood's arrangements got fouled up. Schofield's force marched right by the Confederate outposts during the night of Nov. 29-30 and entrenched at Franklin to the north.

Furious over his missed opportunity, Hood rashly attacked Schofield Nov. 30 at Franklin, which is 18 miles south of Nashville. Repeated assaults failed to dent the Union lines but cost Hood losses of more than 6,000 men. Included were five generals and many other officers Hood would need in the future battle with Thomas.

Hood won the field when Schofield pulled back into Nashville, but the Confederates were badly shaken. Nevertheless Hood pushed on northward and took position on high ground south of Nashville to dig in. We now know it would have been sensible for the Confederates to retreat, but to the pugnacious Hood such a backward step was inconceivable. There was danger his army might

This monument in Nashville National cemetery was erected in 1920 in memory of Minnesota soldiers buried there who were killed in the Civil war. The remains of more than 50 killed in the battle of Nashville lie in the cemetery, along with dead of the Second and Third Minnesota and other units. Sculptor was John K. Daniels.

Minnesota Historical Society

disintegrate if he didn't press forward.

But even Hood now realized he could not attack Nashville with any propect of success. The army Thomas was putting together at Nashville was at least twice as large as Hood's and was protected by some of the strongest fortifications to be set up in any American city. (Nashville, founded in 1779 on the Cumberland river, was popularly known as "the Athens of the South" because of its schools and many buildings in classical Greek style. It had about 30,000 people when the war started, but after the Federals occupied the city in February 1862 its population zoomed to about 100,000. It was a vital supply center for Union troops in the western theater.)

Hood did not have enough troops to besiege Nashville, nor did he dare bypass the city. He decided to wait in his trenches for Thomas to make a move. In other words, Hood's policy now was the passive defensive, which Napoleon called "a form of deferred suicide."

Perhaps the most important reinforcements Thomas was to receive arrived at Nashville from Missouri by Dec. 1. They were two divisions of veteran troops under bluff, hard-fighting Gen. Andrew Jackson Smith. Formerly of the 16th army corps, Smith's divisions were now officially designated a detachment of the Army of the Tennessee.

The Fifth, Seventh, Ninth and 10th Minnesota regiments were all part of the first division of Smith's detachment. At head of the division was Gen. John McArthur (not to be confused with

Maj.—later Gen.—Arthur MacArthur, father of Gen. Douglas MacArthur).

The 10th Minnesota, commanded by Lt. Col. Samuel P. Jennison of St. Paul, was in the first brigade of McArthur's division. Col. William L. McMillen, an Ohioan, led the brigade. Jennison, later of Red Wing, was in charge of the 10th Minnesota because its colonel, James H. Baker of Mankato, had been placed in command of the post of St. Louis, Mo., and was unable to obtain release from his duties there.

The Fifth and Ninth Minnesota regiments were in the division's second brigade, commanded by the Fifth's colonel, Lucius F. Hubbard of Red Wing. Hubbard had headed the Fifth Minnesota regiment at Corinth, Vicksburg and elsewhere. With Hubbard in charge of the brigade, Lt. Col. William B. Gere of Chatfield commanded the Fifth Minnesota.

The Ninth Minnesota was led by Col. Josiah F. Marsh of Preston. As lieutenant colonel of the regiment, Marsh had distinguished himself at Brice's Cross Roads (Guntown), Miss., June 10, 1864. On that occasion he directed the Ninth Minnesota's stout rear-guard fighting that prevented Confederate Gen. Forrest from capturing even more men than he did in a battle that was a complete Union fiasco.

The Ninth's soldierly colonel, Alexander Wilkin of St. Paul, led a brigade at Guntown and also did well there. Wilkin was killed at Tupelo, Miss.. July 14, 1864, when a force commanded by Gen. Smith got a measure of revenge against Forrest.

Col. Lucius F. Hubbard of the Fifth Minnesota commanded a brigade at Nashville.

Lt. Col. William B. Gere commanded the Fifth Minnesota both days of the battle.

Col. William R. Marshall of the Seventh Minnesota also commanded a brigade.

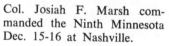

Col. Josiah F. Marsh commanded the Ninth Minnesota Dec. 15-16 at Nashville.

Lt. Col. George Bradley led the Seventh Minnesota after Marshall took over brigade.

Lt. Col. Samuel P. Jennison, who led the 10th Minnesota, was severely wounded.

Wilkin gave his name to a Minnesota county.

The Seventh Minnesota regiment was part of the third brigade (led by Col. Sylvester G. Hill, an Iowan) of McArthur's division. Thus the four Minnesota regiments were in three different brigades. Colonel of the Seventh Minnesota was William R. Marshall, who had been a pioneer merchant in St. Anthony and was a St. Paul newspaper publisher when war broke out. Among many Minnesotans with Smith who had fought the Sioux on the frontier, Marshall would serve as Minnesota's fifth governor from 1866 to 1870.

So much for the dramatis personae of Minnesota "brass" with Smith's detachment. Smith's "guerrillas" were a seasoned, cocky lot. The general knew they could get a bit unruly. When another general complained to Smith that his men had stolen four of six turkeys collected by the headquarters cook, Smith answered: "Couldn't have been my men, not my men; they would have taken them all!"

That the soldiers had confidence in "old A.J." is shown by the following quote attributed to one of Smith's veterans: "We're A. J. Smith's guerrillas. We've been to Vicksburg, Red river, Missouri and about everywhere else . . . and now we're going to Hades if old A. J. orders us."

Before going to Nashville, the men must have felt they were almost following Smith "to Hades." The Minnesotans and others marched a grueling 800 miles all over Missouri to counter a raid being made in that state by Confederate Gen. Sterling Price. After that they marched to St.

Louis, boarded steamers and proceeded to Nashville by way of the Mississippi, Ohio and Cumberland rivers.

The Minnesotans and the rest of Smith's force settled into trenches on the right of Thomas' strong defensive network at Nashville. The Union line arched several miles from the Cumberland river east of the city to the river again west of the city. The Union positions crossed and commanded the eight principal roads that fanned out from Nashville. From west to east they were the Charlotte, Harding, Hillsboro, Granny White, Franklin, Nolensville, Murfreesboro and Lebanon turnpikes (see map).

In a much shorter line to the south, Hood had only three corps, commanded by Generals Alexander P. Stewart, Stephen D. Lee and Benjamin F. Cheatham. Most of the Confederate force was between the Hillsboro pike and the Nolensville pike, a thinly held line five miles long.

Already badly outnumbered, Hood contrived "a masterpiece of suicidal folly" (as Stanley Horn puts it) by sending Forrest off on a railroad-destroying raid toward Murfreesboro, Tenn., 28 miles southeast. Commanding a force that consisted mainly of his cavalry and Gen. William B. Bate's division of Cheatham's corps, Forrest on Dec. 7 had a sharp fight near Murfreesboro with two Union brigades under Gen. Robert H. Milroy.

In one of the brigades was the Eighth Minnesota—called the "Indian regiment" by the others because it had seen long and arduous service against the Sioux. The Eighth's colonel, Minor

T. Thomas of Stillwater, commanded one of the two brigades. Although the Union troops were pulled back into Murfreesboro, Forrest was repulsed. The Eighth Minnesota lost 13 killed and 77 wounded in 30 minutes. One of the wounded was its immediate commander, Lt. Col. Henry C. Rogers of Austin, who later became secretary of state. Men of the Eighth felt they had made amends for Forrest's capture of the Third Minnesota regiment at Murfreesboro in July 1862. Bate's men got back to Nashville in time to do battle nine days later with other Minnesota troops, but Forrest did not return to Hood's lines. The Confederate commander could have used him.

One other Minnesota regiment was stationed near Nashville at the time—the newly-formed 11th, commanded by Col. James B. Gilfillan of St. Paul, afterwards chief justice of the state

Minneapolis Tribune Map

supreme court. The 11th guarded the Louisville and Nashville railroad in the vicinity of Gallatin, Tenn., northeast of the Tennessee capital. Thus six of Minnesota's 11 regiments in the Civil war were stationed in or near Nashville before and during the battle.

Back at Nashville, the deliberate Thomas prepared for battle with characteristic thoroughness. He would not move until his cavalry, commanded by Gen. James H. Wilson, had sufficient mounts. Finally, Thomas was ready to strike Dec. 9, but a storm blew in and covered the Nashville area with a sheet of ice. Movement was impossible, so Thomas had to wait. On Dec. 12, Col. Hubbard wrote his Aunt Mary Hubbard of Chester, Vt.: "The weather the past few days has been very severe, cold and stormy; hence much suffering is entailed upon the troops, who are necessarily much exposed in the trenches." He added that the enemy probably suffered in greater degree. (He was right, since many of Hood's men were barefooted and bareheaded.)

Thomas' delays greatly irritated Washington authorities and Gen. Grant. Overestimating the seriousness of Hood's threat, Grant and others kept prodding Thomas to attack. Refusing to budge until his preparations were completed and the weather cleared, Thomas was on the verge of being replaced. Then the ice melted, and on Dec. 15 Thomas checked out of his Nashville hotel room, paid the bill and at last ordered a general assault on Hood's lines.

Thomas' plans, carefully outlined to each corps

commander, called for the Union left to feint at the Confederate right (Cheatham's corps) beyond the Nolensville pike, while the Union right made the main attack on Hood's weak left (Stewart's corps) in the vicinity of the Hillsboro pike. Chosen to make the chief assault—in the form of a general left wheel—were Smith's detachment (including the four Minnesota regiments) and Wilson's cavalry, which was stationed on the far right of the Union line.

"Masterly" is the word several historians have had for Thomas' tactics, which worked out just about as planned.

In this artist's drawing, the Seventh Minnesota and the rest of its brigade (the third of McArthur's first division) are shown storming a strong Confederate position— Redoubt No. 3—near the Hillsboro pike during the first day at Nashville. The brigade commander, Col. S. G. Hill (perhaps shown falling off his horse at right), was killed. Col. William R. Marshall of the Seventh Minnesota then led the brigade.   From Harper's Weekly

Fog delayed the feint on the right until 8 a.m., Dec. 15. The main assault didn't get started until about 10 a.m., but then it worked like a charm. Wilson's cavalry (sporting devastating new Spencer repeating rifles) and McArthur's division formed in the vicinity of the Charlotte and Harding pikes.

In his "The Decisive Battle of Nashville," Stanley Horn describes what happened next: "The Federal attacking force swept through the wedge of territory between the Harding and Hillsboro pikes like a giant wheel, with Wood at the hub, Smith along the spoke, and the fast-moving cavalry on the rim . . . " (Gen. Thomas J. Wood's corps, Thomas' largest, formed the Union center.)

The cavalry and Smith's infantry drove Stewart's men on the left from their redoubts and entrenchments and by nightfall Hood's entire army retreated to the south to form a shorter line, some three miles wide, on the Overton hills near the Granny White and Franklin pikes.

In the Dec. 15 assault, the 10th Minnesota was on the right of McArthur's division and helped take an isolated work called Redoubt No. 5. Other Minnesota regiments assailed other positions (like Redoubt No. 4) and helped carry them, capturing many prisoners. The Seventh Minnesota, on the left of McArthur's division, took Redoubt No. 3 along with the rest of the third brigade. Nearby Confederate gunners then fired on this redoubt. Long afterwards, Capt. Theodore G. Carter of St. Peter, a member of the Seventh Minnesota's

This rare photograph, taken before 1900, shows Shy's hill as it may have looked at the time of the battle. The picture apparently looks west across the Granny White pike. Confederate troops took position behind the stone fences. Today Shy's hill is being "invaded" by homes.

company K, wrote in the publication, "Confederate Veteran," that "the gunners cut their fuses so that every shell burst inside of it (the redoubt), and there did not seem to be 10 seconds' interval between the discharges. Col. S. G. Hill, our brigade commander, gave the order to charge the fort on the hill, and was shot through the head the next moment. Our major heard the order and repeated it; we jumped down from the wall and, led by Col. Marshall, crossed the pike and climbed the hill, the Confederates leaving the fort as we got to it." Marshall from then on led the third brigade during the battle and Lt. Col. George Bradley, who lived at Belle Plaine and Forest City before the war, commanded the Seventh Minnesota.

Both sides bivouacked on the battlefield the night of Dec. 15-16. The shorter line to which Hood's men retired was about two miles behind the position of Dec. 15. Anchoring the Confederate left was Shy's hill, named after Col. William Shy of the 20th Tennessee regiment, who was killed there Dec. 16. Gen. William B. Bate's

116

division, which had fought against the Eighth Minnesota at Murfreesboro Dec. 7, dug in on top of the hill, located between the Hillsboro and Granny White pikes. Bate's men were part of Cheatham's corps, which had been moved from the right to the Confederate left during the night.

The pattern of fighting on Dec. 16 was much the same as the day before. The Confederate right beat back an attack (this time much more spirited), after which disaster developed on the left, as on Dec. 15.

Early on the 16th, Smith's corps groped for the enemy and stopped 600 yards away. McArthur's division was on the right in front of the key Confederate position—Shy's hill.

Bate's men on the hill were shelled from three sides during the day. From noon on, both armies were pelted by a cold rain. Gradually Wilson's dismounted cavalry got around to the Confederate rear and fired their deadly repeaters. They posed a serious threat.

At about 4 p.m., apparently acting on his own initiative, McArthur ordered his three brigades to attack Shy's hill frontally. The men had to advance some 400 yards over open, muddy fields "exposed to the deadly range of the enemy's guns" (said Hubbard), before they could go up the hill. Stone walls and fences were in the way.

McMillen's first brigade, with the 10th Minnesota on the left of his first line, led off. When it was halfway up the hill, Hubbard's second brigade (with the Fifth and Ninth Minnesota forming his first line) followed. Although he

117

received no order, Marshall (on the left) took up the charge when he saw Hubbard moving on his right. The Seventh Minnesota was on the left of Marshall's first line.

With bayonets fixed, all three brigades charged up the hill toward the Confederate fortifications. The men did not stop to fire; they kept moving. A Confederate volley went over the heads of most of McMillen's brigade when it neared the enemy parapets, but the 10th Minnesota was punished severely. Lt. Col. Jennison fell wounded near the top. "Nothing daunted, this gallant regiment, to-

Adapted from map in "The Decisive Battle of Nashville."

gether with the others composing the front line, cleared the enemy's works with a bound," reported Col. McMillen.

The three brigades swept over the Confederate works, seizing guns, battle flags and hundreds of prisoners. The Confederate left gave way as other troops took up the attack. Then the center and the right broke for the rear. Says Stanley Horn: "The Federals' successful assault on the Confederate position on Shy's hill was the decisive factor in this decisive battle."

What was left of Hood's army retreated as rapidly as possible. The Confederates had been routed as they had never been in the entire war. Henry Ahsenmacher of Le Sueur, a sergeant in the 10th Minnesota's company G, summed it up in his diary: "Our attack had the force of a lion, and the Rebels could do nothing but flee before us like wild sheep."

After the war, men of the four Minnesota regiments at Nashville never could agree about which outfit planted its colors first on the parapets, or which captured the most prisoners. One thing, though, was sure: they had done honor to their state and their regiments.

Gen. John McArthur, commander of the Minnesotans' division, had kind words for his men in various reports after the battle. To Abraham Lincoln he reported Dec. 17 that "Smith's 'guerrillas' again did a noble work yesterday, not the least portion of which is due the first division."

In a postscript to a later report, McArthur said: "I wish particularly to mention . .   the gallant conduct of Col. W. R. Marshall, Seventh Minnesota infantry volunteers, commanding third brigade, called to take command during the first day's battle and continuing throughout. His admirable management and example stamp him as an officer of rare merit."

Col. Hubbard was personally complimented by Generals Thomas, Smith and McArthur for the charge of his brigade, and the three telegraphed Lincoln their recommendation that Hubbard, among others, be appointed brigadier general.

The color bearers of all four Minnesota regiments were shot down several times during the charge. The Fifth Minnesota had three color bearers killed and four of the color guard wounded.

Hubbard suffered a neck wound and had two horses shot under him. The wounded Jennison, Hubbard and Marshall all were b r e v e t t e d brigadier general for their work at Nashville. Besides becoming future governors, Hubbard and Marshall also gave their names to Minnesota counties. So did Michael Cook of Faribault, major of the 10th Minnesota, who died Dec. 28 of wounds suffered at Nashville.

In the spring of 1865, Minnesota's four "Nashville" regiments, plus the Sixth, took part in a campaign to take Mobile, Ala.

And what of Hood's army? Some of it escaped capture during the flight from Nashville because of the skillful rear-guard fighting of Forrest's cavalry. The irrepressible nature of Civil war soldiers, both north and south, somehow seemed to be summed up by the following ditty that Hood's men sang to "The Yellow Rose of Texas" as they retreated across the Tennessee river:

*So now we're going to leave you, our hearts are
    full of woe;*
*We're going back to Georgia to see our Uncle
    Joe.*
*You may talk about your Beauregard and sing
    of General Lee,*
*But the gallant Hood of Texas played hell in
    Tennessee.*

Sixth Minnesota's "pest-hole": Camp Buford, Helena, Ark.

HARDSHIP AT HELENA

IT WAS THE LOT of most of Minnesota's 11 Civil war regiments to achieve sufficient glory in combat to atone for camp drudgery and to be represented in a painting at the Minnesota state capitol.

The Sixth Minnesota, through no fault of its own, was less fortunate. In June 1864 it moved from the healthy Minnesota-Dakota frontier, where it fought well against the Sioux in 1862-3, to the heat and swamps of Helena, Ark.—"a malaria-stricken, disease-fostering hole," as the regimental historian put it. The regiment was 940 strong when it arrived in Helena June 23. Almost at once malarial fevers felled many of the men, but the regiment was stuck there until Nov. 4. During the stay of little more than four months at Helena,

122

72 men of the Sixth Minnesota died and more than 600 were sent to northern hospitals. Six weeks after the regiment's arrival at Helena, only seven officers and 178 enlisted men reported fit for duty. Finally sent to St. Louis Nov. 11, the regiment took a creditable part in the Mobile, Ala., campaign near the war's end. Says historian William W. Folwell: "The country should ever remember that the (nearly) fourscore men who died of fever at Helena were as deserving of its gratitude as if they had fallen in battle."

CHRONOLOGY

Minnesota in the Civil War and Sioux Uprising of 1862.

1861

April 14 Gov. Alexander Ramsey of Minnesota was in Washington the day after Fort Sumter, S. C., surrendered. He offered 1,000 men for national defense—the first tender of troops from any northern state.

April 15 President Lincoln called for 75,000 volunteers to serve three months. Ramsey telegraphed Lt. Gov. Ignatius Donnelly in St. Paul to call for volunteers. That night the St. Paul Pioneer Guards met and Josias R. King was the first to sign up. This gave him claim to being the first volunteer in the United States service in the Civil war.

April 29 Ten companies of the First Minnesota regiment were mustered in at Fort Snelling. Willis A. Gorman was named colonel.

May 10 The First Minnesota was reorganized as a three-year outfit. It claimed to be the senior three-year regiment for the north. On May 3 Lincoln had called for 42,000 three-year volunteers.

July 21 A month after leaving home, the First Minnesota got its first taste of combat at the battle of First Bull Run (Manassas), Va., a Union defeat. The Minnesotans lost 42 killed, 108 wounded and 30 missing while taking part in an attempted turning movement of the Confederate left. Unlike most regiments, the First Minnesota left the field in good order.

Oct. 14 The newly organized Second Minnesota regiment embarked at Fort Snelling for Washington. On the way its orders were changed and it was sent to Kentucky. Its colonel was Horatio P. Van Cleve.

Oct. 21 At the battle of Ball's Bluff, Va., northwest of Washington, the First Minnesota performed valuable service during withdrawal of Union troops across the Potomac river after another northern setback. Minnesotans manned boats.

Nov. 17 The newly organized Third Minnesota regiment left Fort Snelling by steamer for duty in the south. Its colonel was Henry C. Lester.

1862

Jan. 19 The Second Minnesota, under fire for the first time, played an important part in the Federal victory at Mill Springs, Ky., under Gen. George H. Thomas.

The regiment lost 12 killed and 33 wounded in the battle, also known as Logan's Cross Roads.

March 9 The famous duel between the ironclads Monitor and Merrimack (Virginia) ended in a stand-off at Hampton Roads, Va. Among other things, the wooden frigate Minnesota was saved from destruction.

April 6 The First battery, Minnesota light artillery, helped hold the Hornets' Nest long enough to prevent a complete Federal rout on the first day of the battle of Shiloh, Tenn. Union forces turned the tide the next day. The battery lost three killed and eight wounded during its heroic stand at Shiloh.

April 20 The Fourth Minnesota regiment, after service at frontier forts, embarked for St. Louis, Mo., under command of Col. John B. Sanborn. It became part of the Army of the Mississippi.

May 24 The seven companies of the newly organized Fifth Minnesota regiment not engaged in frontier service at home were sent south to join in Gen. Henry W. Halleck's "slow motion" siege of Corinth, Miss. Also taking part in the move on Corinth were the Second and Fourth Minnesota regiments and the First Minnesota battery.

May 28 The Fifth Minnesota regiment lost three killed and 12 wounded in the battle of

Farmington, Miss., before Corinth fell at the end of May.

May 31 As part of Gen. George B. McClellan's Army of the Potomac, the First Minnesota regiment participated in the Peninsular campaign aimed at Richmond, Va., and on this day held an important position against a Confederate attack at Fair Oaks (Seven Pines), Va., 10 miles east of Richmond. The battle was inconclusive.

June 29 Fighting an important rear-guard action during a Seven Days' battle of the Peninsular campaign, the First Minnesota lost 48 killed or wounded at Savage's Station, Va.

June 30 The First Minnesota lost several more wounded in another Seven Days' battle at Glendale, Va. (also known as Frayser's Farm, or White Oak Swamp).

July 13 The Third Minnesota regiment was surrendered at Murfreesboro, Tenn., to raiders led by famed Confederate cavalry leader Gen. Nathan Bedford Forrest. Later, Col. Henry Lester and all other officers who voted for surrender were dismissed from the service.

Aug. 17 Four young Sioux Indians murdered five settlers in Acton township of Minnesota's Meeker county and thereby triggered the Sioux uprising of 1862 in the four-year-old state. From 400 to 800 whites met death in the ensuing days and several counties were depopulated.

Aug. 18 Indians under Little Crow attacked the Lower Sioux agency on the Minnesota river, killing traders and other white men at the agency and taking several women and children captive.

Troops of the Fifth Minnesota from Fort Ridgely on the other (north) side of the river headed for the agency and were ambushed at Redwood Ferry. Capt. John Marsh, in command of the force, drowned and half of his 46 men were killed.

Indians killed many settlers along the Minnesota and Cottonwood rivers and near creeks on the north side of the Minnesota.

Indians attacked the Upper (Yellow Medicine) agency near the mouth of the Yellow Medicine river about midnight.

Aug. 19 The first attack on New Ulm, Minn., was beaten off by townspeople and others. Friendly Indian John Other Day led Upper agency fugitives to safety with a long trek to Henderson, Minn.

Aug. 20 The first Indian attack on Fort Ridgely, Minn., was repulsed by troops stationed there and by civilians who flocked to the fort.

Aug. 22 The main attack on Fort Ridgely failed. A sizable relief force under Col. Henry H. Sibley arrived at St. Peter, Minn., from Fort Snelling.

Aug. 23 The major attack on New Ulm was repulsed by several units of citizen soldiers under Judge Charles E. Flandrau. Nearly 200 of the frontier town's buildings were destroyed.

Aug. 28 Sibley's relief force arrived at Fort Ridgely.

Sept. 2 A burial party of soldiers and others was ambushed at Birch Coulee, some 13 miles west of Fort Ridgely. Indians finally were beaten off the next day after severe fighting.

Sept. 3 Whites and Indians fought a skirmish called the battle of Acton near where the Sioux uprising started. Indians raided Hutchinson and Forest City, Minn., and Fort Abercrombie on the Red river.

Sept. 17 In a crucial battle of the Civil war at Antietam (Sharpsburg), Md., the First Minnesota regiment lost heavily (147 men killed or wounded) during an attack on the Confederate left and center. At this time the regiment was led by Col. Alfred Sully and conducted itself well. It was one of the regiments of the first brigade (commanded by Gen. Willis A. Gorman, the First Minnesota's first colonel), of the second division (Gen. John Sedgwick), of the second corps (Gen. E. V. Sumner) of the Army of the Potomac, then led by Gen.

George B. McClellan.

Sept. 19 The Fourth Minnesota regiment was actively engaged in the minor but hotly contested Union victory at Iuka, Miss., losing three killed and 44 wounded. This was the Fourth's first battle. The Fifth Minnesota was on the field but was held in reserve in this battle.

Sept. 23 A force of about 1,600 troops, led by Sibley, defeated Indians under Little Crow at Wood Lake near Yellow Medicine, ending organized Indian attacks in Minnesota. Sibley's army included all, or parts of, the Third, Sixth, Seventh and Ninth Minnesota regiments and the Renville Rangers. The Third Minnesota bore the brunt of the battle. Only one company of the Ninth was present.

Sept. 26 Many Indians were captured and 269 white and half-breed captives of the Indians were freed at Camp Release near the mouth of the Chippewa river above present-day Montevideo, Minn.

Sept. 28 to Nov. 5 A military commission tried nearly 400 Indians in the field. More than 300 were sentenced to be hung.

Oct. 3-4 The Fourth and Fifth Minnesota regiments and First Minnesota battery of light artillery took part in the battle of Corinth, Miss. The Fifth in particular distinguished itself by helping turn the tide of battle with an attack on Confederates who had penetrated the Union

131

lines. The Fifth regiment lost seven killed and 16 wounded in the battle; the Fourth, two killed and 10 wounded.

Oct. 8 The Second Minnesota regiment was lightly engaged in the important but indecisive battle of Perryville, Ky., which ended the Confederate invasion of Kentucky. The Second Minnesota battery of light artillery had six wounded while fighting all day at Perryville.

Dec. 13 The First Minnesota regiment had but two officers and 13 men wounded at Fredericksburg, Va., while most regiments of the second corps were subjected to senseless slaughter in one of the worst Union defeats of the war.

Dec. 26 Thirty-eight Indians and half-breeds were executed at Mankato, Minn., for crimes committed in the 1862 Sioux uprising. President Lincoln had greatly reduced the list to be killed, much to the dislike of Minnesota's aroused populace at the time. Episcopal Bishop Henry B. Whipple counseled moderation and helped get the Indians a fairer break than they otherwise would have had.

1863

**Dec. 31
1862
to
Jan. 2,** The Second Minnesota battery lost some 10 men killed or wounded in the bitterly fought but inconclusive battle

1863 of Stones River (Murfreesboro), Tenn.
April 29 The Fourth Minnesota regiment, the
to Fifth Minnesota and the First Minne-
July 4 sota battery took part in most of the
actions that marked the brilliant Vicksburg campaign of Gen. Ulysses S. Grant.
On May 22, when the siege of Vicksburg, Miss., was in progress, the Fourth
Minnesota lost heavily (12 killed and
42 wounded) in a futile attack along
with other Union troops on the Confederate stronghold's fortifications.

June 8 The Third Minnesota regiment, back
down south after helping quell the Sioux
uprising at home, became one of the
regiments taking part in the siege of
Vicksburg. Its main role was to help
keep a Confederate relief force under
Gen. Joseph E. Johnston from reaching
Vicksburg from the northeast.

June 23 The Second Minnesota regiment parti-
to cipated in the Tullahoma campaign in
June 30 Tennessee which helped prevent Confederates under Gen. Braxton Bragg
from moving to the aid of Rebels besieged at Vicksburg to the west.

July 2 Late in the second day of the climactic
battle of Gettysburg, Pa., the First
Minnesota regiment lost a record 82
per cent of its 262 men during a sacrificial charge against two Confederate
brigades. Only 47 escaped and 215
lay dead, dying or wounded after the

133

charge. Gen. Winfield S. Hancock, commander of the second corps, ordered the attack to gain five minutes' time to bring up reserves at a critical moment. He said later: "There is no more gallant deed recorded in history."

July 3 On the third and last day of the battle of Gettysburg, the First Minnesota lost another 17 killed or wounded in the repulse of Pickett's famous charge against the Union center on Cemetery ridge.

Back in Minnesota on this day, Sioux Chief Little Crow was shot and killed by settlers near Hutchinson while he was on a horse-stealing foray.

July 4 The Fourth Minnesota, with its division, led troops that entered Vicksburg when that Gibraltar finally surrendered. The Fourth stayed on as part of the occupation force and had many men die of sickness, particularly malaria.

July 10 Gov. Alexander Ramsey resigned to become United States senator and was succeeded by Henry A. Swift, who had been president pro tempore of the senate. Swift had been acting lieutenant governor since March 4, when Ignatius Donnelly resigned that office to go to congress.

July 24 to July 28 A punitive expedition led by Gen. Henry H. Sibley (he was promoted after the battle of Wood Lake) fought a series of battles or skirmishes with the Sioux Indians at Big Mound, Dead Buffalo Lake and Stony Lake near present-day Bismarck, N. D. Sibley's force included the Sixth, Seventh and 10th Minnesota regiments, the Minnesota Mounted Rangers and artillery. Indian warriors fought delaying actions long enough to permit their women and children to escape across the Missouri river. The expedition succeeded in driving the Indians westward but not in capturing them.

Aug. 13 The Third Minnesota regiment marched from Helena, Ark., in intense heat and started on a campaign to expel Confederates from Arkansas. The regiment spent the rest of the war (about two years) in Arkansas, losing more than 100 men by disease but seeing little fighting.

Aug. 23 to Sept. 6 The First Minnesota regiment was one of the units sent to New York City to prevent recurrence of draft riots there.

Sept. 11 The Third regiment entered Little Rock, Ark., and became part of the occupation force there. Colonel of the regiment at this time was Christopher C. Andrews. He was detailed as commander of the post of Little Rock.

Sept. 19 The Second Minnesota regiment lost eight killed and 41 wounded near Jay's mill in the opening encounter of the

135

large-scale, bloody battle of Chickamauga, Ga.

Sept. 20 The Second Minnesota suffered heavy
losses at Kelly's field in helping repel
a Confederate attack during the second
day of the battle of Chickamauga. Later
in the day the regiment performed heroic
service as it and other units held Snodgrass (Horseshoe) ridge long enough
to allow most of the defeated Union
army to escape to Chattanooga, Tenn.
At Chickamauga, where Gen. George
H. Thomas earned the nickname of
"Rock of Chickamauga" thanks in part
to the Second Minnesota, the Minnesotans' total losses were 45 killed, 103
wounded and 14 captured—162 casualties out of 384 men engaged.

Oct. 7 After months of frontier duty, the
Seventh Minnesota (commanded at various times by two future governors,
Stephen Miller and William R. Marshall) was sent south to St. Louis, Mo.

Oct. 14 The First Minnesota captured 322 Confederates in helping turn back Gen.
Robert E. Lee's attempted flanking
movement at Bristoe Station, Va. The
Minnesotans lost one killed and 16
wounded.

Oct. 26
to A prominent Minnesotan, Gen. William
G. LeDuc of the quartermaster corps,
Oct. 30 helped open the "cracker line" so food
could get through to hungry Union

136

troops (including the Second Minnesota) besieged at Chattanooga.

Nov. 25 The Second Minnesota and the rest of Gen. George H. Thomas' Army of the Cumberland charged up Missionary ridge south of Chattanooga and routed the Confederates who held the ridge. It was a "soldier's battle" not ordered by generals in command. The regiment lost eight killed and 31 wounded in the victory at Missionary ridge.

Nov. 26 to Dec. 1 The First Minnesota took part in the Mine Run (Va.) campaign—its last—a probing movement by the Army of the Potomac across the Rapidan river.

1864

Jan. 11 Stephen Miller, who had risen to the rank of brigadier general in war service, took over as governor of Minnesota. In his message as retiring governor, Henry A. Swift pointed out that claims amounting to $2,458,000 had been filed as a result of Indian raids.

Feb. 5 Since most of the First Minnesota members' three years of service had expired, the regiment was ordered home. It was honored Feb. 6 at a grand banquet at National hotel in Washington.

Feb. 29 Home on furlough after re-enlisting for three years, the Second Minnesota regiment was honored at a grand reception and ball at the Winslow hotel building

137

in St. Anthony.

Mar. 10 to May 22 The Fifth Minnesota regiment conducted itself creditably as part of the futile Red river expedition in Louisiana under Gen. Nathaniel P. Banks.

April 1 The Third Minnesota regiment lost seven killed and 16 wounded in the relatively minor battle of Fitzhugh's Woods near Augusta, Ark. It was a Union victory and put a stop to Confederate recruiting in the area.

April 29 The First Minnesota was mustered out at Fort Snelling, except for men who re-enlisted in t w o companies t h a t formed the First Battalion, Minnesota Infantry Volunteers. T h e battalion's story is a continuation of the First Minnesota regiment's distinguished record. The battalion took part in the final campaigns in the east.

May 6 to Sept. 1 The Second Minnesota regiment and First Minnesota battery took part in Gen. William T. Sherman's Atlanta campaign that led to the fall of Atlanta, Ga., Sept. 2.

June 10 The Ninth Minnesota regiment, which had seen frontier service and had been ordered south in Oct., 1863, participated in the Union fiasco at Brice's Cross Roads (Guntown), Miss. The victorious Confederate cavalry was led by Gen. Nathan B. Forrest. The Ninth Minnesota's spirited rear-guard fighting

138

for three days probably saved the Union force of 8,000 from capture. The Ninth lost nine killed, 33 wounded and 233 as prisoners of war. Most of the enlisted men were sent to the notorious Rebel prison at Andersonville, Ga., where 119 soon died. Others were permanently broken in health.

June 14 The Sixth Minnesota regiment, after nearly two years of frontier service, left Fort Snelling for duty in the south. It had the misfortune to be stationed at Helena, Ark., where it fought a serious battle against disease, not Rebels. During slightly more than four months at Helena, 72 men died and some 600 were sent to hospitals.

July 14 At Tupelo, Miss., men of four Minnesota regiments got a measure of revenge against notorious Confederate cavalry leader Gen. Nathan B. Forrest by helping defeat him. Only a small part of the Fifth regiment was present, but the Seventh regiment was engaged to the extent of having 10 killed and 52 wounded in the Federal victory. The Ninth Minnesota played a minor role but lost its fighting colonel, Alexander Wilkin, the highest ranking soldier from Minnesota to be killed during the Civil war. Josiah F. Marsh became the Ninth's colonel. The 10th regiment, which also had seen frontier service and was the last of the

139

regiments organized in the late summer of 1862, lost one man killed and 12 wounded at Tupelo.

July 28 The Eighth Minnesota regiment, and cavalry and artillery units from the state, took part in the battle of Killdeer Mountain in Dakota territory. Gen. Alfred Sully was in command during the battle, one of the major engagements of the Sioux war.

Sept. 3 The Fifth, Seventh, Ninth and 10th Minnesota regiments joined in a grueling 800-mile march in pursuit of raiding Confederate Gen. Sterling Price in Missouri. The Minnesotans did little or no fighting in the campaign but they performed some of their hardest service in the war nevertheless.

Oct. 5 The Fourth Minnesota, under Lt. Col. John E. Tourtellotte, was part of the Union force that repulsed a vigorous Confederate attack at Allatoona Pass, Ga., some 40 days before Gen. William T. Sherman started on his march through Georgia to the sea.

Oct. 26 The Eighth Minnesota, after long and arduous service in the Sioux war, hurriedly left Fort Snelling for Murfreesboro, Tenn.

Nov. Minnesota's Republican majority in the national election of 1864 was smaller than in 1860. The vote stood 25,055 for Abraham Lincoln and 17,367 for

140

Democrat Gen. George B. McClellan.

Nov. 15 The Second Minnesota regiment, the
to Fourth Minnesota and the First Min-
Dec. 21 nesota battery made the march to the
sea to Savannah, Ga., with Gen. William T. Sherman. Savannah fell as a
"Christmas present" for Lincoln.

Dec. 7 The Eighth Minnesota helped repel a
raid on the garrison at Murfreesboro a
week before other Minnesota regiments
fought at nearby Nashville, Tenn. The
Eighth regiment lost 13 killed and 77
wounded in 30 minutes at Murfreesboro, scene of the Third Minnesota's
humiliating surrender two and one-half
years earlier. After this action, the
Eighth Minnesota went east to North
Carolina.

Dec. 15 The Fifth, Seventh, Ninth and 10th
to Minnesota regiments were in the thick
Dec. 16 of key attacks on the Confederate left
both days during the battle of Nashville. On Dec. 16th the four Minnesota
regiments and several others made the
culminating assault on Shy's hill that
shattered t h e Confederate left a n d
forced Gen. John B. Hood's army to
retreat. Commander of Union forces
was Gen. George H. Thomas. Minnesota losses—302 killed, wounded or
missing—were the greatest the state
suffered in any Civil war engagement.

1865

Feb. 1 The Second Minnesota and the rest of Sherman's army (including the First Minnesota battery) began the march through the Carolinas that led to surrender of forces under Gen. Joseph Johnston on April 26. The Second Minnesota marched 480 miles with but minor casualties in this campaign. The Fourth Minnesota also campaigned in North Carolina.

Mar. 17 to April 8 The Fifth, Sixth, Seventh, Ninth and 10th Minnesota regiments took part in the Mobile, Ala., campaign. The city fell near the war's end.

May 24 The Second and Fourth Minnesota regiments and F i r s t Minnesota battery marched with Sherman's army in the grand review before President Andrew Johnson and other government officials in Washington.

July, Aug. Sept. The various Minnesota regiments were discharged at various times at Fort Snelling.

Nov. 11 Sioux chiefs Medicine Bottle and Little Six (Shakopee) were hanged at Pilot Knob near the mouth of the Minnesota river for their part in the Sioux uprising of 1862. They were captured in Canada.

Postcript: Just as Minnesota can lay claim to having the first Union volunteer of the war, it also had the last survivor of the Union army. He was Albert Woolson, 109, who died Aug. 2, 1956, in Duluth, Minn. A statue honors him at Gettysburg, Pa.

Roster of top officers in 11 Minnesota regiments and two batteries of light artillery.

FIRST MINNESOTA REGIMENT
COLONELS:

Willis A. Gorman—Served from April 29, 1861, until Oct. 1, 1861, when he was promoted to brigadier general and commanded a brigade.

Napoleon J. T. Dana—Was colonel from Oct. 2, 1861, to Feb. 3, 1862. Then he was promoted to brigadier general and commanded a brigade.

Alfred Sully—Served as colonel from Feb. 3, 1862, to Sept. 26, 1862, then became a brigadier general and brigade commander.

George N. Morgan—Served as colonel from Sept. 26, 1862, to May 5, 1863, when he resigned because of ill health. Earlier he had been a company captain, major and lieutenant colonel of the regiment.

William Colvill—Was colonel from May 6, 1863, to May 4, 1864, when part of the regiment closed out its three years of service (some men were mustered out April 29). Colvill had been a company captain, major and lieutenant colonel of the regiment.

LIEUTENANT COLONELS:

Stephen Miller—Served from April 29, 1861, to Sept. 16, 1862, when he was made colonel of the Seventh Minnesota. He later became governor.

Charles P. Adams—Served from Sept. 26, 1862, to May 4, 1864. Earlier he was a captain and then major of the regiment.

MAJORS:

William H. Dike—Served from April 29, 1861, to Oct. 22, 1861, when he resigned.

Mark W. Downie—Served as major from May 6, 1863, to May 4, 1864, when he became lieutenant colonel of the First Battalion.

SECOND MINNESOTA REGIMENT

COLONELS:

Horatio P. Van Cleve—Served as colonel from July 23, 1861, to March 21, 1862, when he became a brigadier general and brigade commander.

James George—Was colonel from May 15, 1862, to June 29, 1864. Resigned because of illness. Earlier was lieutenant colonel.

Judson W. Bishop—Was named colonel March 5, 1865, near end of war after having served as lieutenant colonel from Aug. 26, 1862. He frequently commanded the regiment when James George was ill.

146

LIEUTENANT COLONELS:

Alexander Wilkin—Held this rank from May 15, 1862, to Aug. 26, 1862, when he became colonel of the Ninth Minnesota. Earlier he had been a captain in the First Minnesota and resigned to become major of the Second Minnesota regiment Sept. 18, 1861.

Calvin S. Uline—Held this rank late in the war from April 4, 1865, to July 11, 1865.

MAJORS:

Simeon Smith—Served from July 23, 1861, to Sept. 17, 1861, when he was appointed paymaster of the United States army.

John B. Davis—Served as major from Nov. 5, 1862, to April 15, 1864.

John Moulton—Served from April 4, 1865, to July 11, 1865.

THIRD MINNESOTA REGIMENT

COLONELS:

Henry C. Lester—Named colonel Nov. 15, 1861, after serving as a captain in the First Minnesota. Was dismissed Dec. 1, 1862, for the Third Minnesota's surrender at Murfreesboro July 13, 1862.

Chauncey W. Griggs—Named colonel Dec. 1, 1862, and resigned July 15, 1863. Earlier he had been a captain, major and lieutenant colonel.

Christopher C. Andrews—Named colonel July 15, 1863, after serving as a captain and lieutenant colonel. Promoted to brigadier general Jan. 4, 1864.

Hans Mattson—Served as colonel from June 13, 1864, to Sept. 2, 1865. He had been a captain and major and lieutenant colonel of the regiment.

147

LIEUTENANT COLONELS:

Benjamin F. Smith—Served from Nov. 5, 1861, until resignation May 9, 1862.

Everett W. Foster—Named lieutenant colonel April 27, 1864, he resigned May 22, 1865.

James B. Hoit—Served from May 25, 1865, to Sept. 2, 1865. Had been captain and then major.

MAJORS:

John A. Hadley—Served from Nov. 5, 1861, until resignation May 1, 1862.

Benjamin F. Rice—Named major April 27, 1864, he resigned July 20, 1864.

William W. Webster—Became major July 21, 1864, after serving as a captain, and resigned Nov. 12, 1864.

FOURTH MINNESOTA REGIMENT

COLONELS:

John B. Sanborn—Named colonel Jan. 1, 1862, and kept this rank until being promoted to brigadier general Aug. 4, 1863.

John E. Tourtellotte—Named colonel Oct. 5, 1864, after serving as lieutenant colonel from Aug. 24, 1862. Resigned June 21, 1865.

LIEUTENANT COLONELS:

Minor T. Thomas—Became lieutenant colonel Nov. 5, 1861, after serving as a lieutenant in the First Minnesota. Became colonel of the Eighth Minnesota Aug. 24, 1862.

James C. Edson—Became lieutenant colonel Sept. 16, 1864, after serving as a captain and major of the regiment.

MAJORS:

148

A. E. Welch—Became major of the Fourth Minnesota after being wounded and captured at Bull Run as a lieutenant with the First Minnesota. He died at Nashville, Feb. 1, 1864.

Luther L. Baxter—Served from April 10, 1862, until resignation Oct. 10, 1862.

Leverett R. Wellman—Served from June 22, 1865, to July 19, 1865.

FIFTH MINNESOTA REGIMENT
COLONELS:

Rudolph von Borgersrode—Served from April 30, 1862, until resignation Aug. 31, 1862.

Lucius F. Hubbard—Made colonel Aug. 31, 1862, after serving as lieutenant colonel. Remained colonel until brevetted brigadier general Dec. 16, 1864.

LIEUTENANT COLONEL:

William B. Gere—Named lieutenant colonel Aug. 31, 1862, and continued at that rank until Sept. 6, 1865. Was major earlier.

MAJORS:

Francis Hall—Served as major from Aug. 31, 1862, until resignation April 30, 1863.

John C. Becht—Served from May 1, 1863, to March 18, 1865.

John P. Houston—Served from May 10, 1865, to Sept. 6, 1865.

SIXTH MINNESOTA REGIMENT
COLONELS:

William Crooks—Served from Aug. 23, 1862, until resignation Oct. 28, 1864.

John T. Averill—Served from Nov. 22, 1864, until end of war. Was named lieutenant colonel Aug. 22, 1862.

LIEUTENANT COLONEL:

Hiram P. Grant—Served from Nov. 25, 1864, to Aug. 19, 1865, after promotion from a company captain and then major. He was made major April 9, 1864.

MAJORS:

Robert N. McLaren—Served from Aug. 22, 1862, until Jan. 12, 1864, when promoted to colonel of the Second Minnesota cavalry.

Hiram S. Bailey—Served as major from Nov. 25, 1864, until Aug. 19, 1865.

SEVENTH MINNESOTA REGIMENT

COLONELS:

Stephen Miller—Named colonel Sept. 16, 1862, after serving as lieutenant colonel of the First Minnesota. Was promoted to brigadier general Nov. 6, 1863, but soon resigned to become governor.

William R. Marshall—Named colonel Nov. 6, 1863, and served until Aug. 16, 1865. Had served as lieutenant colonel of the regiment after Aug. 28, 1862.

LIEUTENANT COLONEL:

George Bradley—Named lieutenant colonel Nov. 6, 1863, and served to Aug. 16, 1865. Had been promoted to major Sept. 5, 1862.

MAJOR:

William H. Burt—Served from Nov. 6, 1863, to Aug. 16, 1865.

EIGHTH MINNESOTA REGIMENT
COLONEL:

Minor T. Thomas—Served as colonel from Aug. 24, 1862, to July 11, 1865. He had been a lieutenant in the First Minnesota and lieutenant colonel of the Fourth Minnesota.

LIEUTENANT COLONEL:

Henry C. Rogers—He served from Nov. 14, 1862, until discharged for wounds May 15, 1865.

MAJORS:

George A. Camp—Served from Nov. 20, 1862, until resignation May 2, 1865.

Edwin A. Folsom—Served from May 28, 1865, to July 11, 1865.

NINTH MINNESOTA REGIMENT
COLONELS:

Alexander Wilkin—Served as colonel from Aug. 24, 1862, until he was killed at Tupelo, Miss., July 14, 1864. Earlier he had been a captain in the First Minnesota and major and lieutenant colonel of the Second Minnesota.

Josiah F. Marsh—Served as colonel from July 27, 1864, until Aug. 24, 1865.

LIEUTENANT COLONELS:

Josiah F. Marsh—Held this rank from Aug. 24, 1862, until made colonel.

William Markham—Served from July 27, 1864, until Aug. 24, 1865. Had been major from Sept. 15, 1862.

MAJOR:

Horace B. Strait—Was major from July 27, 1864, to Aug. 24, 1865. Earlier was a captain.

151

10th MINNESOTA REGIMENT
COLONEL:
James H. Baker—Served from Nov. 17, 1862, to Aug. 19, 1865.
LIEUTENANT COLONEL:
Samuel P. Jennison—Served from Sept. 10, 1862, to Aug. 19, 1865.
MAJORS:
Michael Cook—Served from Sept. 15, 1862, until death from wounds at Nashville Dec. 27, 1864.
Edwin C. Sanders—Served as major from March 1, 1865, until Aug. 19, 1865. Earlier he had been a captain.

11th MINNESOTA REGIMENT
COLONEL:
James B. Gilfillan—Served from Nov. 3, 1864, to June 26, 1865. Earlier he had been a captain in the Seventh Minnesota.
LIEUTENANT COLONEL:
John Ball—Served from Sept. 7, 1864, to June 26, 1865.
MAJOR:
Martin Maginnis—Served from Sept. 13, 1864, to June 26, 1865.

FIRST MINNESOTA BATTERY OF LIGHT ARTILLERY
CAPTAINS:
Emil Munch—Served from Nov. 7, 1861, until resignation Dec. 25, 1862.
William Z. Clayton—Served from Jan. 1, 1863, to June 30, 1865.

SENIOR FIRST LIEUTENANT:
William Pfaender—Served from Oct. 16, 1861, until he resigned to accept a commission in the Minnesota Mounted Rangers.

SECOND MINNESOTA BATTERY OF LIGHT ARTILLERY
CAPTAIN:
William A. Hotchkiss—Served as captain from Feb. 14, 1862, to Aug. 16, 1865.
FIRST LIEUTENANTS:
Gustave Rosenk
Albert Woodbury
Richard L. Dawley
Henry W. Harder
Alexander Kinkead
George W. Tilton

153

MINNESOTA'S CIVIL
WAR MONUMENTS

AT GETTYSBURG, PENNSYLVANIA

1. A large monument, located on Cemetery ridge near the huge Pennsylvania memorial, commemorates the First Minnesota's charge of July 2, 1863. A sizable granite base is surmounted by a figure of a charging soldier by sculptor Jacob H. G. Fjelde.

2. A smaller granite shaft, on Cemetery ridge just south of the Angle, marks the First Minnesota's position when it helped repulse Pickett's charge July 3, 1863.

3. A small urn, the only one left in Gettysburg National cemetery, marks the area where Minnesota dead are buried. Many other urns of the same type once stood in the cemetery but all except Minnesota's have disappeared.

4. A new memorial to the Grand Army of the Republic features a statue of the late Albert Woolson of Duluth, Minn., last Union veteran of the Civil war. The memorial, for which Avard Fairbanks did the sculpture, was dedicated in September 1956, a month after Woolson's death.

154

AT VICKSBURG, MISSISSIPPI

1. A granite obelisk, more than 90 feet high, commemorates the service of the Third, Fourth and Fifth Minnesota regiments and the First Minnesota battery of light artillery at Vicksburg. Located on Union avenue, the monument has a statue of peace by sculptor William Couper.

2. Small granite markers, with tablets, locate positions of the Fourth and Fifth Minnesota regiments and First Minnesota battery.

AT SHILOH, TENNESSEE

A tasteful memorial to the First Minnesota battery of light artillery is located in the Hornets' Nest-Sunken Road area, where the battery helped stand off Confederate attacks for eight hours April 6, 1862. A life-size statue of an artilleryman by sculptor John K. Daniels of Minneapolis is atop a pedestal against a granite background.

AT CHICKAMAUGA, GEORGIA

1. A medium-size granite monument on Snodgrass hill marks the area where the Second Minnesota regiment and several other units under Gen. George H. Thomas made a stand that saved the Union army Sept. 20, 1863. Atop the monument are three figures—a flag bearer and two other soldiers.

2. Another Second Minnesota monument with a bas-relief of two soldiers stands on the Reed's bridge road north of Jay's mill. It marks the regiment's location when it took part in the opening engagement Sept. 19, 1863, of the two-day ·battle

of Chickamauga.

3. The third (and smallest) monument to the Second Minnesota at Chickamauga is located in Kelly's field where the regiment fought hard and suffered losses Sept. 20 before taking to Snodgrass hill.

4. A modest monument with a ball on top on Viniard field honors the service of the Second Minnesota battery of light artillery at Chickamauga.

AT CHATTANOOGA, TENNESSEE

A granite shaft atop Missionary ridge in what is now a residential area of Chattanooga commemorates the Second Minnesota regiment's part in the successful assault on the ridge Nov. 25, 1863.

AT NASHVILLE, TENNESSEE

An attractive monument, featuring sculptor John K. Daniels' fine statue of a woman holding a wreath, stands in memory of Minnesota Civil war dead buried in Nashville National cemetery.

AT ST. LOUIS, MISSOURI

A monument duplicating the one at Nashville honors Minnesota war dead in Jefferson Barracks National cemetery.

AT ANDERSONVILLE, GEORGIA

A monument with John K. Daniels' figure of a young Union soldier with bowed head stands in memory of Minnesota's Civil war dead at Andersonville National cemetery.

AT MEMPHIS, TENNESSEE

A duplicate of the Andersonville monument honors Minnesota war dead at Memphis National cemetery.

AT LITTLE ROCK, ARKANSAS

Another duplicate of the Andersonville monument honors Minnesota war dead at Little Rock National cemetery.

ELSEWHERE

Minnesota troops are mentioned on several tablets locating Federal units at such battlefields as Antietam, Maryland, and Stones River, Tennessee.

Monuments in Minnesota include one with a Josias R. King statue near the St. Paul cathedral and several marking Sioux uprising sites in and near the Minnesota river valley.

BIBLIOGRAPHY

The manuscripts and newspaper departments of Minnesota Historical society have considerable source material on Minnesota in the Civil war.

Books and articles:

Battles and Leaders of the Civil War. 4 vols. New York, 1884-1888.

Bishop, Judson W., *The Story of a Regiment.* St. Paul, 1890. (History of Second Minnesota.)

Boatner, Mark M. III, *The Civil War Dictionary.* New York, 1959.

Brown, Alonzo L., *History of the Fourth Regiment of Minnesota Infantry Volunteers.* St. Paul, 1892.

Brown, Fred E., *The Battle of Allatoona.* In "Civil War History," September 1960.

Catton, Bruce, *The American Heritage Picture History of the Civil War.* New York, 1960.

Catton, Bruce, *Glory Road.* Garden City, N.Y., 1952.

Catton, Bruce, *Mr. Lincoln's Army.* Garden City, N.Y., 1951.

Catton, Bruce, *This Hallowed Ground.* Garden City, N.Y., 1956.

Downey, Fairfax, *Storming of the Gateway.* New York, 1960.

Folwell, William W. *A History of Minnesota.* 4 vols. St. Paul, 1921-1930. (Volume II is most pertinent.)

Heilbron, Bertha L., *The Thirty-Second State.* St. Paul, 1958.

Hesseltine, William B., *Lincoln and the War Governors.* New York, 1948.

Holcombe, Return I., *History of the First Regiment Minnesota Volunteer Infantry.* Stillwater, Minn., 1916.

Holcombe, Return I., and Hubbard, Lucius F., *Minnesota in Three Centuries.* Volume III. New York, 1908.

Horn, Stanley F., *The Army of Tennessee.* Norman, Okla., 1952.

Horn, Stanley F., *The Decisive Battle of Nashville.* Baton Rouge, La., 1957.

Kunz, Virginia Brainard, *Muskets to Missiles.* St. Paul, 1958.

Miers, Earl Schenck, *The Web of Victory.* New York, 1955.

Military Order of the Loyal Legion of the United States, Minnesota Commandery, *Glimpses of the Nation's Struggle.* 6 vols. St. Paul, 1887-1909.

Minnesota Historical Society Collections. Volume XII. St. Paul, 1908.

Minnesota in the Civil and Indian Wars. 2 vols. St. Paul, 1890-1899.

Mitchell, Joseph B., *Decisive Battles of the Civil War*. New York, 1955.

Stevens, John H., *Personal Recollections of Minnesota and Its People*. Minneapolis, 1890.

Tucker, Glenn, *Hancock the Superb*. Indianapolis, 1960.

Tucker, Glenn, *High Tide at Gettysburg*. Indianapolis, 1958.

War of the Rebellion: *A Compilation of the Official Records of the Union and Confederate Armies*. 128 vols. Washington, 1880-1901. (Several volumes contain Minnesota material.)

Williams, Kenneth P., *Lincoln Finds a General*. 5 vols. New York, 1949-1959.

Wolf, Hazel C., editor, *Campaigning With the First Minnesota*: *A Civil War Diary*. All four issues of "Minnesota History" for 1944.

INDEX

161

Faribault Volunteers, 17
Farmington, Miss., 89
Fifteenth Corps, 78
Fifth Minnesota Infantry
    Regiment, 40, 41, 74, 76-
    79, 81, 83, 85, 87, 89-99,
    101, 107-109, 117, 120
First Minnesota Battery, 74,
    87, 95
First Minnesota Infantry
    Regiment, 15-28, 30, 32,
    33, 61, 64
Fitzhugh's Woods, Ark.,
    Battle of, 60
Fjelde, Jacob H. G., 30
Florence, Ala., 105
Florida Troops, 24
Folwell, William W., 60, 62,
    123
Forest City, Minn., 116
Forrest, Gen. Nathan B., 61,
    62, 103-105, 108, 111,
    112, 120
Fort Donelson, Tenn., 69,
    86
Fort Henry, Tenn., 86
Fort Pemberton, Miss., 77
Fort Pillow, Tenn., 75
Fort Ridgely, Minn., 64, 90
Fort Snelling, Minn., 19, 20,
    28, 54, 64
Fort Sumter, S. C., 15, 86
Forty-third Illinois Infantry
    Regiment, 59
Forty-fifth Illinois Infantry
    Regiment, 71
Forty-seventh Illinois Infan-
    try Regiment, 91
Fourteenth Corps, 45, 46
Fourth Corps, 105
Fourth Minnesota Infantry
    Regiment, 38, 39, 67, 70-

72, 74, 76-84, 88, 94, 95,
    98, 99, 103
France, 91
Franklin, Col. W. B., 20
Franklin Pike, 111, 115
Franklin, Tenn., 105
Frederick, Md., 22

Gallatin, Tenn., 113
Gardner, Alexander, 27
George, Col. James, 49
Georgia, 104
Gere, Thomas P., 90
Gere, Lt. Col. William B.,
    90, 92, 108, 109
Gettysburg, Pa., City and
    Battle of, 15, 17, 18, 21,
    22, 27, 28, 32, 33, 44,
    49, 69, 94, 103
Gilfillan, Col. James B., 112
Glencoe, Minn., 53
Goodhue County, Minn., 59
Goodhue Volunteers, 17
Gorman, Col. Willis A., 18,
    19
Grand Gulf, Miss., 75, 79
Granny White Pike, 111,
    115, 116, 117
Grant, Gen. Ulysses S., 46-
    48, 51, 67, 69, 70, 76-81,
    83, 86, 88, 93, 94, 99,
    101, 104, 113
Green, Charles H., 62
Grierson, Col. Benjamin H.,
    79
Griggs, Col. Chauncey W.,
    63

Halleck, Gen. Henry W., 88,
    89, 93
Hamburg, Tenn., 86
Hancock, Gen. Winfield S.,
    15, 22-26, 28, 29

164

Louisville, Ky., 94, 104

MacArthur, M a j. Arthur,
MacArthur, Gen. Douglas,
    108
Mankato, Minn., 54, 71, 82,
    108
Marsh, Col. Josiah F., 108,
    109
Marshall, Col. William R.,
    109, 110, 114, 116, 118,
    120
Marvin, Matthew, 17, 26
Maryland, 21, 94
Mattson, Lt. Col. Hans, 59,
    66
McArthur, Gen. John, 107,
    108, 110, 114, 115, 117,
    119, 120
McClellan, Gen. George B.,
    94, 95
McClernand, Gen. John A.,
    78, 81
McGrorty, Lt. William B.,
    90, 96
McMillen, Col. William L.,
    108, 117, 118, 119
McMinnville, Tenn., 63
McPherson, Gen. James B.,
    71, 72, 78, 81, 84
Meade, Gen. George G., 22
Memphis & Charleston Rail-
    road, 85, 86, 91, 95
Memphis, Tenn., 75
Mexican War, 19
Millet, Francis D., 39
Milliken's Bend, La., 77
Mill Springs, Ky., 31
Milne, John O., 17, 20, 21
Milroy, Gen. Robert H., 111
Minneapolis, Minn., 19
Minnesota, 15, 18, 56, 63,

65, 69, 85, 87, 96, 102,
    106, 110, 112-115, 119,
    120, 122
Minnesota Pioneer Guards,
    16, 17, 29
Minnesota River, 64
Minnesota State Capitol, 18,
    59, 72, 98, 122
Missionary Ridge, Battle of,
    31, 35, 46-48, 50-53
Mississippi, 44, 65, 76, 79,
    85, 91, 93, 94
Mississippi Central Railroad,
    76
Mississippi River, 19, 55,
    56, 67, 69, 71, 74-77, 86,
    90, 111
Missouri, 56, 107, 110
Mitchell, Joseph B., 26
Mobile, Ala., 120, 123
Mobile & Ohio Railroad, 86,
    96
Morgan, Col. George N., 18
Morrison County, Minn., 17,
    62
Mower, Col. Joseph A., 89,
    92
Mullen, John, 53
Murfreesboro Pike, 111
Murfreesboro, T e n n., 55,
    60-62, 65, 111, 112, 117
Murphy, Isaac, 60

Napoleon, 107
Nashville, Tenn., City and
    Battle of, 42, 43, 61, 87,
    101, 102, 104-107, 109-
    114, 119, 120
Nashville National Cemetery,
    106
Neill, the Rev. Edward D.,
    19

The type used in this book is Times Roman. It was set in a 10 point size and then enlarged photographically to almost a 12 point. The antique headlines are in an authentic Civil War face, called Tuscan Ombre. The book was printed by offset lithography. The color separations were first made for rotogravure and then converted for this use. Printed by Meyers Printing Company, Minneapolis, Minnesota.